For Judith -
All the best!

Mama and Margaret

A. Embry Burrus

PublishAmerica
Baltimore

Flavia quote used by permission ©Weedn Family Trust.

ISBN: 1-4137-5693-X
PUBLISHED BY
PUBLISHAMERICA, LLLP.
www.publishamerica.com
Baltimore

Printed in the United States of America

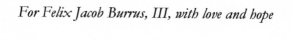

For Felix Jacob Burrus, III, with love and hope

It is the wise and shining spirits in this life who find love in small things, and are richly blessed.
—Flavia

Acknowledgments

I offer the most sincere gratitude to the following people: My mother, who has shown me the true meaning of courage; my precious sister, Margaret, who inspires me every day to become a better person; my writing group—Jill, Julie, Kathryn, Robin and Katie—your support and encouragement has been invaluable; Mary Carol Moran, a wonderful writing teacher; Rebecca, for her wisdom and countenance; all the special people in Margaret's life who love and care for her and who contributed their stories to this book; and to Reita, my good friend and consummate editor who was always willing to listen or to read—thank you for helping me believe in myself as a writer.

Prologue
As Good as it Gets

I WAS THIRTY-EIGHT YEARS OLD and had just finished graduate school. Feeling like I'd spent a large part of my adult life wasting time, now that I'd discovered my passion in life, I was ready to get down to business. *I need to move to a big city*, I thought. *I'm not getting any younger.*

I received my master's degree in speech-language pathology from Auburn University, a big school in a picturesque little town in East Central Alabama. Prior to graduate school, I had changed cities almost as much as I had changed jobs. At one point, I moved 700 miles from everything that was familiar to me, leaving my small town Georgia roots for the beautiful beaches of Miami.

I had received my B.S. degree from Auburn some fifteen years earlier and thought it would be nice to return to my alma mater, earn a post-graduate degree and finally do something with my life. Not that I had been a bum or anything, I had always been able to find a job. I just never felt like I was making a difference—a tiny voice inside of me kept nagging, *you can do better.* At the same time, I was being drawn closer to home. Mama was in her late seventies and had overcome breast cancer and congestive heart failure. And of course, there was my beloved sister Margaret who has Down syndrome. I had been away from them for long enough. With all of those things in mind, I decided that Atlanta would be the ideal place for me to spread my wings and conquer the world.

About midway through my graduate program, I came to the decision that I wanted to work in a medical facility of some kind, preferably a hospital. My "calling," I decided, was to work with stroke victims or people with head trauma. "I want to work with adults," I told one of my classmates, "and the last place I'd ever want to work," I arrogantly stated, "is in the public schools."

When someone from Egleston Children's Hospital came to speak to our class, however, I began wavering. Her job sounded extremely challenging, yet fascinating and very rewarding. I was immediately drawn into her world and changed my mind about working with adults. Even more attractive was the fact that Egleston Hospital was in Atlanta. Two months later, I applied and was accepted for an externship at one of their outpatient clinics. Everything was working out perfectly.

The experience I gained at Egleston had a profound affect on me. Realizing that I enjoyed the challenge of working with children, I expressed my desire to stay on at the clinic if there was a position available. Unfortunately there wasn't, and I was tossed headfirst into the sea of young (and not so young) professionals looking for work in Atlanta.

I applied for a position with Emory University hospital, Scottish Rite children's hospital, Dekalb Medical Center and even a nursing home, but none of them offered me a job. Even though they liked me and thought I was knowledgeable, I didn't have a license and at the time, that was a major drawback.

When you finish a master's degree in speech pathology, you have to complete a clinical fellowship year, also called a CFY. During the first nine months of your employment, no matter where you work, you must be supervised for a specific number of hours by someone with a license. Once you complete the nine months, pass the national exam and receive sign-off from your supervisor, *then* you can apply for a license. All of the places I applied were looking for someone had already jumped through the hoops.

After several months of interviews and rejections, I came

across an ad in a trade magazine for contract work. It read: *Atlanta area, great pay, summers off, will hire CFY.* I swallowed hard, summers off could only mean one thing. Wondering how many ways one could prepare crow, I dialed the number from the ad. I had one interview with a nice lady named Janice Moore. A few weeks later, she mailed me a contract and I was employed by her company. My first job, of all places, was going to be in the Atlanta public schools. I laughed at the irony of it all, the way the universe puts you right where you need to be, even if you say (right out loud I might add) that it's the last place on earth you'd like to be.

Five days before I was to start my new job, I received a letter from Janice. *You have been assigned to Camp Creek Middle School,* it read. *Please report at eight a.m. on August seventeenth.*

The next day, a Friday, I bought a map and found my way to South Atlanta. The school was in a somewhat rural area close to the airport. A sprawling, one-story brick building, it seemed nice enough. *This isn't so bad,* I thought. *Barring any accidents on the interstate, it's only thirty minutes from home.* Little did I know that a thirty-minute drive would transport me, and my way of thinking, to another world.

With the exception of a few children, the majority of Camp Creek's enrollment consisted of residents from two of the most dangerous housing projects in South Atlanta. One of them was so unsafe, the city decided to evacuate the residents and tear the place down. Many of these children had witnessed more violence before the sixth grade than I would see in a lifetime. School was by far the best thing these kids had going for them—structure, discipline and two meals a day.

Within weeks, I grew to love every child who walked through my door, realizing that if I wanted to give something back, if I truly wanted to save the world, this was a good place to start.

The next nine months proved to be life altering for several reasons: what I learned about myself, what I learned about the children I worked with, and most surprisingly, what I learned about Margaret.

11

Because Camp Creek was a one-story building and centrally located, there were over 100 children with disabilities enrolled there. I had children with a multitude of diagnoses on my caseload—autism, hearing impairment, behavior disorder, learning disability, cerebral palsy and severe mental retardation. And even though there were several children in the school with Down syndrome, oddly enough, none of them qualified for speech therapy.

"Why aren't these kids on my caseload?" I asked the senior speech therapist.

"Because they're not eligible for services," she responded.

"Why not?"

"Well, they're mostly non-verbal for one thing and secondly, their cognitive skills are too low. Their speech and language skills are as good as they're going to get."

I stared with what I'm sure was a blank look on my face.

Reading the look on my face she continued. "Most of these kids don't have any home life. Either their families don't care about them or they're too poor and uneducated to know better."

Stunned, I thought, *How could their families not care about them? Why aren't they like Margaret?*

At thirty-eight, I had never met a person with Down syndrome who couldn't communicate or who didn't lead some semblance of a normal life. It was suddenly very clear to me how fortunate my sister was; how much it mattered that she and most of her peers had grown up in a loving, nurturing, stimulating environment. That day, something changed in me, and I looked at life, especially Margaret's life, from a different perspective.

During the Christmas break of that same year, without any clue as to how to go about it, I began writing the story of Margaret's life. I sat at my computer for several days in a row, re-creating the story from memories of our childhood. My motivation at the time was to tell some funny stories and also to preserve my sister's memory. I wanted to make sure that future generations of our family would know about Margaret. I wrote for a few hours each day and hacked out about ten or fifteen pages in a week's time. *I've started a book,* I thought. *I'm on a roll.* Then, after the New Year, I headed back to work. The writing slowed down, life started up, and little by little, I lost interest.

Four years later, I moved back to Auburn to take a job as a clinical professor in the program from which I had graduated. After mentioning to one of my colleagues that I was writing a book (yeah, right), she introduced me to her friend Jill Davis. Jill, who was writing a memoir as well, told me about a writing class that would be starting the following January. *This is your chance,* I thought, *make a commitment.* I signed up for the class and the rest, as they say, is history, or more aptly, divine providence.

Each week, my classmates and I spent the first hour learning about writing and the next two hours exposing our souls to each other—we were encouraged to bring at least six to ten pages to read aloud. The class, along with our esteemed teacher, Mary Carol Moran, a published novelist and poet, would provide positive, yet constructive critique. A scary prospect at first, it proved to be the jump-start I needed. With Mary's direction and the encouragement of my fellow writers, my once disjointed prose began to morph into something real, something actually worth reading.

Writing a book is not just about the end product, it's about how the experience of writing transforms your world. For me, it was an astounding revelation: *As a child, I was never aware of my sister's disability.* Margaret was no different from anybody else. She was just Margaret, my big sister, my best playmate, my closest friend. We laughed and cried, shared secrets and fought and made up, just like siblings in any typical family. In fact, for a long time, Margaret could do anything that I did, and some things, she did even better. We had each other and in our world, that was all that mattered.

What I didn't, or couldn't, understand at the time was that all of these things were true because of our mother. Mama believed that Margaret should have the same opportunity as anyone else, therefore, it was so. We didn't spend our childhood going to therapists, specialists or support groups—Mama was all of those things rolled into one. And so over time, the truth was revealed. The story that had to be told was not just about one special person, it was about two—the story was about Mama and Margaret.

Awakening

SOMEHOW MAMA KNEW SHE WOULD BE the one to endure the stares and sweat through the awkward moments when she took her baby out into the world. Mama was the one who had to deal with her own fear while facing the fears of everyone with whom she came in contact. Daddy was at work when Mama went to the grocery store, the park, the library or to pick Jake up from school. Even if Daddy had been around, he wouldn't have allowed himself to see how people responded or didn't respond. Only a mother could cope with such blatant rejection; a mother, that is, who had been entrusted with a significant task.

Of course there were always those people who weren't afraid of Margaret, those who would actually look at her and smile, those who didn't feel uncomfortable around her, not knowing what to say. A few were adults, but most of the people who regarded Margaret as a fellow human being were children, and one in particular accepted her unconditionally.

I found this out on a Sunday afternoon some forty-six years after my sister was born. That was the day Mama opened up.

For the most part, it was a Sunday like many others. I made the forty-five minute trip from my home in Auburn across the Chattahoochee River to Columbus to spend the afternoon with Mama and Margaret. We had developed somewhat of a routine—we ate lunch, went for a walk or shopped, depending on the weather or the circumstances, then visited for a while before I drove home late in the afternoon.

This particular day, however, was different. I was at a place in my writing where I needed to ask Mama some very difficult questions; the kind of questions I knew no one had ever asked before.

After we finished lunch, Margaret went into the den to watch television. Mama and I sat alone at the beautiful dining room table that had once belonged to her mother. Our conversation had drifted from family to work, and finally, to the dreary weather outside. I figured this was as good a time as any.

"Mama," I said, "I want to ask you some questions about when Margaret was a baby."

"Like what?" she responded, awkwardly busying herself with the fringe around her place mat.

"Well," I continued, "I was wondering how people responded to her, you know, how they reacted when they saw her."

Mama looked past me out the window. Her eyes searched briefly for something before coming to rest again on the table in front of her. Suddenly I was struck by this beautiful woman sitting across from me. I noticed her long, thin fingers, the glint of silver in her short wavy hair, the skin that bore so few wrinkles. Mostly, though, I noticed the sadness in her eyes, a sadness that had never been mentioned, and probably, never even acknowledged. My mind raced. *Maybe I shouldn't do this.*

"Do you remembuh the Smiths?" Mama started in her slow, deliberate cadence.

"I don't think so," I said. "Why?"

"They lived down the street from us on Bolton Avenue," she said. "Their oldest son Ken played on Jake's baseball team, so we'd always see his mother and younger brother Phil at the games." Mama paused. "Of course I always had to take Margaret with me, she was just a baby."

I tried to digest her statement. *Of course, I had to take Margaret with me.* A picture flashed through my mind of proud, smiling mothers eagerly showing off their bundles of joy. Sadness engulfed me as I imagined what my mother must have felt.

"Phil always wanted to hold Margaret," Mama continued. "Every time he saw her, he asked if he could hold her."

"How old was Phil?" I asked.

"Oh, I guess he was about three or four. He was always so sweet to Margaret, and just a little bitty thing himself."

I could imagine Phil wanting to hold Margaret. By all accounts, she was adorable when she was little; a mop of white blond hair and hazel eyes that danced when she smiled, and she was always smiling. I wondered how anyone could pass by her and not want to talk to her or at least ask her name, but I had to remind myself, that's how people act around babies who are perfect, not babies who have Down syndrome.

"Why do you think Phil liked holding Margaret so much?" I asked, forcing myself back to the conversation.

Mama looked up at me, a faint smile played on her lips. "I don't know," she said, "he just did."

I had taken for granted all these years that everyone who encountered Margaret felt blessed to be in her presence, the same way I did. Up until this conversation, I had assumed that Mama felt that way too, but I was operating from my own frame of reference—that of the younger sister who had been adored by the older sister her entire life. Selfishly, I never thought about what life must have been like for my mother.

"How did other people at the baseball park respond to Margaret?" I asked.

Mama paused. The smile had vanished, her voice now barely above a whisper. "Well," she said, "most of them acted like she wasn't there."

I didn't ask Mama how that made her feel. I wanted to, but I knew she wouldn't be able to tell me. Even if she could name the emotion, she would be reluctant to talk about it. That's just how Mama is.

I'd been aware of my mother's reticence for a long time, but only since I started writing this book have I realized just how much she's held inside, the myriad of emotions she's never talked about. Mama would never admit and, more than likely, isn't even aware of the courage it took to raise a child with Down syndrome in a time when society often chose to look the other way. She never focused on those things. And she never would have talked about any of this if I hadn't asked her to. No, my mama would never tell the story herself, so that's why I started writing, because the story begged to be told.

The Gift

MY BIG SISTER CAME INTO THE world on a cold January morning, 1958. She was small, weighing only five pounds six ounces, but Dr. Reynolds, Mama's obstetrician, performed the customary slap on the bottom and pronounced her a healthy baby girl.

Mama and Daddy had decided that if their long awaited second child was a girl, they would name her after Mama's aunt Margaret, her daddy's only sister. She was the person Mama admired most in the world. The baby's middle name, whether a boy or a girl, would be Andrews, Mama's maiden name.

As soon as she was delivered, Margaret was whisked out of the cold, sterile room to be poked and prodded and given the final once-over before any formal introductions could be made; standard practice for newborn babies in 1958. And according to Mama, until the nurse brought Margaret into the room to see her for the first time, nobody had noticed that anything was wrong.

My part in all of this is that I came along only two short years later—talk about an unplanned pregnancy. I had a brother who was eleven and a two-year-old sister with Down syndrome. Mama was forty-one; Daddy was two months away from forty-two, and only ten years away from his first heart attack. At least it wasn't a stroke, which is what our housekeeper, Katie Mae Baker, used to talk about when Margaret and I were toddlers. She'd plop herself down in our big rocking chair, pull us onto her knee and exclaim, "Lawd have mercy, you chullen gon' gimme a stroke."

Felix Jacob Burrus, Jr. (Jake), our big brother, was born in December 1948—three days after Christmas. I've always thought that people who are born around Christmas really get gypped on their birthdays. A card stuck to your present that reads, Merry Christmas, oh and by the way, Happy Birthday too.

Mama said she always took the decorations down the day after Christmas so Jake would feel special. To this day, that's one of the sweetest things I've ever heard my mama say.

Jake was Mama and Daddy's first child and the apple of his Mama's eye. Quiet and unassuming, bright and talented; a sweet, thoughtful boy—what some folks might refer to as the second coming.

As Jake got older, Mama wanted to have another child, at least one more. You see, my daddy was an only child and, according to Mama, downright spoiled rotten. She was determined that her son wasn't going to suffer the same fate.

So when Jake was about four years old, Mama and Daddy began the process of trying to get pregnant again. After a couple of years with no success, they considered adoption, but in the 1950s, adoption was difficult if you already had one child. Besides, Mama said she couldn't stand those people meddling around in her personal life. Mama's never been one to tell anybody her business, friends and family included, so she wasn't about to tell it to a stranger.

They forgot about adoption and almost five years later, when Mama had all but given up on saving Jake from ruin, the news came—a baby was on the way.

Throughout my adulthood, I'd wondered what it was like for Mama and Daddy when Margaret was born. So many questions ran through my head: *Who said what? How did they feel? Did they even talk about it at all?* It wasn't until I decided to start writing things down that Mama and I had a serious conversation about my sister.

20

I had come to visit for the weekend. Mama was up early as usual and I joined her at the breakfast table. Margaret wouldn't stir for another hour or so. Mama, still wearing her nightgown and robe, read the paper and sipped coffee. I felt nervous, like I was fifteen and about to ask permission to go on a weekend trip with no chaperone.

"Mama?" I said, tentatively.

"Yes, dahlin'."

"How did you feel when Margaret was born...you know, when you found out?"

Never taking her eyes off the paper, she said, "I was scared."

"What about Daddy?"

"I think he was scared too," she said. Mama laid the paper down on the table and stared into her coffee cup. "He didn't want to talk about it with me, but evidently he had talked to Mr. Hooten."

I vaguely remembered that name from my childhood. "Who was Mr. Hooten again?" I asked.

"He was your daddy's boss when Margaret was born."

"Oh yeah. Wasn't he the one who got Daddy started as a mechanic?"

"Yes, that was him," she said. "And unfortunately, your daddy hung on his every word."

"So, what did Mr. Hooten say to Daddy?"

"Well, he told him that we shouldn't even take Margaret home from the hospital, that we should send her to an institution right away."

I don't think I could have realized until that moment how difficult the situation must have been for Mama and Daddy, how helpless they must have felt. "What did you say when Daddy told you that?" I asked.

Mama made eye contact with me for the first time during our conversation. Her voice was strong, determined. "I said, she's my baby and I'm taking her home."

"What did Daddy say then?"

"Well, he didn't say anything. I don't think he knew what to say."

Mama's head was bowed again. She folded and refolded her already crumpled napkin, then picked up her cup, took a long drink and continued. "I know he was upset, though, because after we brought Margaret home from the hospital, he'd walk the streets at night. Your daddy was very distraught over having a mentally retarded child."

"Wasn't that hard for you?"

"Well, yeah, I guess," she said. "But I knew worrying about it wasn't going to do any good. Besides, I thought if God gave her to me, He must think I'm capable of taking care of her."

With that statement, Mama ended our conversation, but there would be many more to follow. Through this process, I would learn so much about my mother and father—their struggles, their victories, their fears. But what I would find most inspiring is the courage it took for my parents, and many others like them, to persevere against so many odds, not knowing what lay ahead. How Mama, in particular, overcame fear, doubt, even desperation in order to ensure the best possible life for her child with special needs.

As I wrote, an affirmation bore into my brain, a mantra that I would come to accept as an explanation for Margaret's presence in our family, a simple, undeniable truth: *God gives special children to special people.*

The Good Doctor

WHEN MARGARET WAS BORN, AND EVEN as late as the 1970s, doctors routinely cautioned parents of babies born with Down syndrome not to take their children home from the hospital. Those same doctors might have tossed around phrases like "Mongoloid idiot" and doled out unsolicited, devastating advice: *Your child will never walk or talk. He probably won't live past the age of five. She's going to have all kinds of medical problems. Have her sent to an institution, that way, you won't get attached.*

Fortunately, no doctor ever said those things to Mama. The doctor who delivered my sister hardly said anything at all other than, "It's a girl." No one on the delivery room staff, including the doctor, noticed anything different about Margaret.

"I don't think they looked at her long enough to know," Mama said. "But I knew. I knew as soon as they showed her to me."

It wasn't until our new neighbor, a young pediatrician named Walker Rivers, examined Margaret that anyone other than Mama noticed something different about her baby. Even though he bore devastating news, this man's presence in our lives was nothing short of a miracle.

Born into a destitute family in Greenville, South Carolina, Walker Rivers grew up during the Depression. His parents moved him and his two siblings around extensively during his childhood, shuffling them between family members as far away as Texas when they had no place to live or not enough money to feed their children. According to one of his daughters, Walker had a very difficult and unhappy childhood.

In spite of the challenges he faced, Walker became an excellent student. He was a bright, thoughtful young man, an overachiever by anyone's estimation. When he was in high school, Walker was invited to attend a reception honoring the school's top students. While there, he met a local philanthropist who was so impressed by Walker, he offered to pay his way to Presbyterian College, a small liberal arts school in nearby Clinton, South Carolina. In college, as was the case in high school, Walker finished at the top of his class. His professors urged him to apply to Harvard, but Walker knew there was no way, even if he was accepted, that he could afford to go to one of the Ivy League's most prestigious schools.

"You're a bright student, Walker," they told him. "Harvard would be lucky to have you." Sure enough, Harvard accepted Walker and as fate would have it, the same man who had paid his way through college, offered to pay Walker's way through Harvard medical school.

"Who was that man?" Walker's children asked him many years later.

"I can't tell you his name," he said. "That was part of our agreement. He asked that I never reveal his identity. His only request was that I give something back through my work. That I make my life my ministry."

Dr. Rivers' wife, Jane, also a doctor, had enrolled at Duke at the age of fourteen and graduated from Yale medical school. They met in New York at Belleview Hospital and married shortly thereafter. Deciding they wanted to return to the South, Walker took a job in Columbus at an established practice that was looking for a young associate. Somehow, his family ended up in the house next door to ours. Walker Rivers wasn't just a doctor, a neighbor or a friend—he was a guardian angel.

A soft-spoken man, Dr. Rivers was tall and handsome with large hands and a gentle touch. For as long as I can remember, he wore a full beard and wire framed glasses. He was the epitome of a family doctor; he cared deeply about his patients and their well-being. He took an interest in his patients' lives, not just their illnesses. When his children got chicken pox, he called Mama and told her to bring us over so we could all share a piece of chewing gum.

"Might as well get it over with, Augusta," he told her. "It'll be easier on everyone if they have it at the same time."

Dr. Rivers was the only person Mama went to for advice regarding Margaret's diagnosis. She didn't consult a specialist or do any research. She didn't talk to other parents or take Margaret for testing. She never read as much as one book about Down syndrome. She trusted Dr. Rivers and liked what he had to say. He passed on his gift, and Mama accepted.

Before Margaret, Dr. Rivers had never treated a child with Down syndrome. He could just as easily have been one of those doctors who said frightening, horrible things to parents with imperfect babies, but he wasn't. He was thoughtful, caring, and compassionate. Instead of instilling fear, he provided hope in a time of great uncertainty.

"What should we expect?" Mama asked him.

"Well, Augusta, I really don't know what to tell you," he said. "I don't know what she will or won't be able to do. I think you should just look at *anything* she does as a milestone."

Dr. Rivers' advice was the best anyone could have given Mama, but even he couldn't have imagined the path Margaret's life would take. What neither he nor Mama knew was that Margaret was smart, healthy and feisty, and she was going to do just about anything she damn well pleased.

Over the Threshold

"Mama, what do you mean you can't remember how old she was when she started talking?"

"Now, honey, that was over forty years ago," Mama drawled. "Besides, I'm eighty-four years old. You should've started writing sooner if you expected me to remember things like that."

No, Mama doesn't remember Margaret's first word, or how old she was when she uttered it. As frustrated as I was, I had to remind myself that to Mama, this was no big deal. Babies crawl, then walk, then start talking, simple as that.

The only thing Mama remembers about Margaret's developmental milestones is that at some point Jake became very curious about his baby sister.

"I don't remember exactly when it happened," Mama said, "I just remember that Jake asked me when she was going to start walking."

Margaret must have known her big brother was wishing for a playmate, because it wasn't long before she stood up and took her first steps. Once she got the whole forward momentum thing figured out, Margaret didn't slow down. She toddled around behind Mama, Jake, even the dog. Soon, she'd have some real competition though—a person her own size to contend with.

Over the years, Mama's alluded to the fact that I provided

motivation for Margaret; that my presence encouraged her overall development, but I know different. Margaret was already walking and talking just fine by the time I came along, she didn't need me for anything. As I think back on our childhood, it's obvious to me that Mama was the reason for Margaret's achievements—my sister's "normalcy" had nothing at all to do with me. It was based solely on the fact that Mama knows only one way of responding: *Don't complain and don't ask for help. Do the best you can with what you've been given.*

As I steered our conversation that day toward my parents' reaction to the arrival of a third child, I was more or less prepared for Mama's response. My unexpected arrival had been a topic of many conversations in the past. I was not, however, prepared for what was to follow.

"I was shocked when I found out I was pregnant with you," she told me. "I thought I was going through the change of life."

"What did Daddy think about having another child? I asked.

"I really don't know what your daddy thought, honey, but I know it was hard for him because he wanted to be the center of attention."

As difficult as it was to hear Mama say that, I wasn't shocked. Daddy was always distant, now I knew why. Since Mama had opened the door, I stepped over the threshold and posed a question that no child ever wants to ask a parent.

"Do you think Daddy even wanted to have children?"

Mama looked at me and paused. When she spoke, her tone was thoughtful, but sincere. "I know he loved y'all," she said, "but your daddy expected me to worship at his feet. The truth of the matter is he was jealous. Y'all took me away from him and he didn't like that one bit."

My heart felt heavy, my breath caught in my chest. I felt sad, not for myself or Jake or Margaret, but for Mama. When she found out she was pregnant with me, she must have questioned everything in her life. She was forty-one years old with a selfish husband and two children, one with disabilities. I can't imagine how hurt, isolated and afraid she must have felt.

That's when I realized that the love and attention I received from Margaret sustained me during the first several years of my life. Daddy was distant and detached, Jake lived in his own world, and Mama did all she could just to hold it together. She spent every day trying to forge a family out of five individuals and it took all the physical and emotional energy she had.

If not for our beloved housekeeper, Katie Mae Baker, Mama may as well have been raising three children by herself. Although she would never admit it, Mama needed someone to lean on. She didn't confide in Katie or seek her advice, yet the two of them shared an unspoken kinship—Katie was perhaps the only person who truly understood what Mama was going through. Unfortunately, the color of their skin would prevent Mama from ever calling her housekeeper a friend, but Katie was probably the best friend Mama ever had.

Powder and Biscuits

ALMOST AS WIDE AS SHE WAS tall, with beautiful light brown skin and kind eyes, Katie Mae Baker had a personality as big and sweet as her physical presence. Any room she entered was filled with Katie Mae.

Mama and Daddy lucked into Katie—they inherited her really. After they married, Mama and Daddy moved in with my Grandmother Burrus. Because Daddy was an only child, and his father had died, his mother insisted that her only son and his new wife live with her. A few years later, my Grandmother Burrus had a stroke and was confined to a wheelchair. She hired Katie to be her housekeeper, and, according to Mama, a nursemaid as well.

"What exactly did Katie do for Mrs. Burrus?" I asked Mama. We always called our grandmother "Mrs. Burrus." To this day, I've never heard her referred to by any other name.

"She nursed," Mama said.

"She was a nurse?" I asked.

"No, Katie was just there to serve at your grandmother's beck and call."

Katie knew nothing about modern-day nursing. What she did know was how to take care of folks and cook. Her specialty was something she called a ho-cake. A fried pancake smothered in butter that was so good, you could gain five pounds just smelling it. Katie would become famous in our house for her ho-cakes because they were Jake's favorite, and Katie delighted in pleasing Jake.

Even though she was hired to take care of my grandmother, Katie fell hard for Jake and assumed the role of raising him. With a head full of curly blonde hair and big blue eyes, Jake was the cutest, sweetest little white boy Katie had ever laid eyes on. She doted on Jake, bathing him, dressing him and singing him to sleep every afternoon. Jake stole Katie's heart. Throughout his life as an only child, she was his and his alone.

"Katie used to stand Jake up on the kitchen counter and make him dance the 'Hucklebuck,'" Mama said one day as she reminisced about life before I was born.

"What's that?" I asked.

"That's a dance that was popular way back when." Mama smiled as her mind went back fifty years. "Oooh and Jake just loved it," she said. "Katie worshipped Jake and he loved her to pieces."

Wishing I had been the object of Katie's affection I quickly retorted, "I guess Jake really did have it made before Margaret and I came along."

"Well, he was my first and I didn't know any better," Mama said. "I'm not saying it was right, but Katie and I did everything but breathe for Jake. We anticipated his every want or need and I don't know who was worse, me or Katie."

After my Grandmother Burrus had to be moved into a nursing home, Katie found herself out of a job. By this time, Margaret had come along, so with two children and Daddy to take care of, Mama had her hands full. For once, she was willing to ask for help and proposed that Katie continue on with our family. Katie would have a job and Mama would have life support.

What I remember about Katie is sitting in her lap in a rocking chair next to the fireplace in our den. On a nice day, she'd drag me, Margaret and the rocking chair out to the carport so she could keep an eye on everyone in the neighborhood. My most distinct memory of Katie though was her wonderful smell.

Crawling into her lap, I was engulfed in a mix of powder and biscuits. Katie provided refuge, not only for me and Margaret, but for Mama as well. She eased the burden Mama felt and loved all of us like we were her very own.

"You know, Katie never married or had any children," Mama said, "but I don't think that mattered to her."

"You think she was happy just taking care of us?" I asked.

"I can hear her now," Mama said. "'Miss Gusta, these here's all the chullen I need.'"

Idol Worship

MARGARET WAS THE BEST BIG SISTER anyone could ask for. I'll never have to wonder how she felt about having a younger sibling. Daddy's countless home movies of us tell the story—she dressed me, held me and petted me like I was her very own baby doll. Margaret loved me and I loved her and we were virtually inseparable.

Our big brother, however, was another story. Eleven years my senior, Jake was practically a grown-up by the time I was aware of his existence. Once I was old enough to appreciate him, he had moved out of the house and into the life of a grown man. From my childlike perspective, he could do no wrong, which more than likely led to unfair comparisons and something resembling idol worship.

He was a wonderful big brother to me and Margaret, though, despite the fact that he was an only child until he was nine years old and had the world on a string. He maintains that he was happy about the arrival of his siblings, but I can only imagine how his carefree, serene childhood must have been upended.

Before we came along, Jake spent his time in Cub Scouts, playing in the creek near our house, or building and flying model airplanes with Daddy; his was the perfect boy's life. Then, within three years' time, the family dynamics changed drastically—not one, but two babies to deal with, and girls at that. He did his share of changing diapers, feeding us, playing with us, and even babysitting when Mama and Daddy went out on a Saturday night to play bridge. Not the way a thirteen-year-old boy would choose to spend his weekends. But, according to Mama, Jake never complained.

He was sweet and thoughtful, all the things a big brother should be. When I was three or four, Jake would take turns putting me, and then Margaret in the basket of his bicycle and riding us around the neighborhood. He had a huge square basket attached to his handlebars that he used to hold newspapers for his morning paper route. With the attention of my big brother, I was on top of the world. As Jake pedaled up and down the street in front of our house with me in the basket, Margaret would tag along behind, laughing and calling out "my turn, my turn."

Jake grew apart from us after he started high school, which could only be expected, but he still let us in on parts of his life that were sacred and should have been off-limits to little sisters.

When Jake was seventeen, he started singing in a rock and roll band that would hold practice sessions in our living room. I have no idea how he got Daddy to go for that. Daddy was convinced that the only real music was classical music and he didn't want to come face to face with anything that might prove him wrong. Not to mention, Daddy was an excellent musician and it drove him crazy to hear fledglings hitting the wrong note or strumming the wrong chord.

Jake, on the other hand, was much more tolerant. Most nights that his band practiced, he'd let Margaret and me sit on the floor and play captive audience. Sometimes, he'd even talk the other guys into letting us bang on their drums or even the piano. He introduced us to his friends and made us feel important. To us, there was no bigger thrill and we knew we had the best big brother in the world.

Spinach

THROUGHOUT MOST OF OUR CHILDHOOD, Margaret and I shared a bedroom. Both of the houses we lived in growing up had three bedrooms—one for Mama and Daddy, one for Jake, of course, and one for me and Margaret. We had matching twin beds and matching furniture, and the line of demarcation was clearly drawn—my stuff on one side of the room, Margaret's on the other.

I didn't mind sharing a room with Margaret, but I wanted bunk beds instead of twin beds. I expressed my desire to that end on a regular basis, but even though I begged and pleaded, we never got them. I dug my own grave when I tried convincing Mama that the furniture in our bedroom was causing us to lose popularity points with the other kids in the neighborhood.

"Do you always have to keep up with the Joneses?" Mama asked.

"No, but the Gauses have—"

"The Gauses? What do they have to do with anything?"

"Winky and Kenneth, they have bunk beds," I whined.

"I don't care what they have," Mama preached. "If Winky and Kenneth Gause jumped into the Chattahoochee River, would you jump too?"

That was Mama's standard response to most everything and

much to my chagrin, no further explanation was offered. Frustrated to no end, I would talk back, get a spanking, cry and then sulk. Margaret, on the other hand, was able to suppress her frustration with Mama, but she didn't hold back when I did something to make her mad. Like the time she was walking through the house bent over sideways looking at her new shoes.

Whenever Margaret got a new pair of shoes, she put them on and paraded around the house observing them from every angle. She couldn't just sit in a chair and admire them, she had to see them walking. So, when I walked into the hall that day and bumped into her, she lost her balance and fell down.

"Look what you made me did," she exclaimed.

Grammar has never been one of Margaret's strong suits. To this day she confuses verb tenses.

"I didn't make you do anything. You tripped!" I yelled back.

She reached out and whacked me on the arm. I reared back to return the favor and that's when Mama came into view; spanking number two for me within a matter of hours.

As mad as I would get about the whole situation, I never stayed mad at Margaret for very long. She was too lovable and sweet and she was always, always there when I needed her.

We were just kids. I couldn't have been more than nine or ten. I had been staring at the spinach on my plate for at least thirty minutes. I was praying for something to save me from that spinach. We always had to clean our plates, no questions asked. Sometimes, the dog would eat some unwanted food from my outstretched hand under the table, but on this particular night, Buddy was outside. It was just me, Mama, Margaret and that heinous spinach staring me in the face.

Mama got up to clear some dishes and I hatched my plan. I would put the food on Margaret's plate. I thought to myself, *She'll eat it, she eats everything!*

I shoveled it onto her plate with one hand while putting my finger over my mouth with the other. She started eating it and didn't say a word. I was ecstatic. I couldn't believe it had been that easy. I smiled and thought, *She's such a good sister.*

Mama had noticed that Margaret's plate was clean before she got up to take the dishes. She was standing in front of the stove.

"Margaret, there's some more spinach. Do you want some?"

"No, ma'am."

"Why not?" Mama asked.

"Embry just gave me hers."

No Counseling, No Medication

MY FIRST REAL MEMORY OF MARGARET was when she was about six years old and Mama found her under the bed sharing a package of Rolaids with our dog. Duchess recovered in a day or two. Margaret had diarrhea for a week.

I always knew Margaret was special, but I never thought of her as different. I remember getting very upset the first time the neighborhood kids picked on her. They made fun of her glasses, called her retarded, and mocked and imitated her speech. Confused and upset by their taunting, I went to Mama for an explanation.

"Why are they making fun of her?" I said.

"Well, probably because she's different," Mama calmly replied. "Margaret can learn to do anything, honey, she just might be a little slower at it than most people."

Armed with that information, I became very protective of my big sister. I would jump to her defense at a moment's notice, although Margaret never needed my help at all. Nothing we encountered growing up seemed to have an affect on her. She has gone through life oblivious to adversity of any kind, even Mama's constant preaching. Margaret only pays attention to what really matters—getting to bowling on time or a second helping of mashed potatoes.

Mama didn't find it necessary to explain to me why Margaret was different. As far as she was concerned, the only thing I needed to know was that Margaret was expected to follow the rules just like everybody else. Mama spent most of her time making sure we knew right from wrong. She stayed on both of us constantly, and I'm quite sure she pioneered the phrase, "teachable moment."

"Y'all remember what I told you now...pretty is as pretty does. Young ladies shouldn't act ugly."

Mama's chastising was never really directed at Margaret, she didn't act ugly. That was my job. Margaret did whatever Mama said and didn't question anything—never talked back, never asked why, nothing. However, since the two of us were usually together, she had many opportunities to learn vicariously through me. By the time she was four years old, Margaret was practically the most well-behaved child in the state of Georgia. Next to me, her impeccable manners shone even brighter, and mine, well, they always needed more polish.

"I don't want to hear you say 'yeah' again," Mama would say. "You say 'yes, ma'am' or 'yes, sir.' Do you understand me?"

This seemed trivial to me. What difference did it make? Of all the things she could get mad at me about.

I walked to my room, sullen. "Yes, ma'am," I said as I moped down the hall.

Margaret followed me into the bedroom and tried to comfort me as only she could.

"It's okay, Embry. She didn't mean to."

"Yes, she did," I whined.

"You need to do what I do," she said. "I just say 'yes, ma'am' or 'yes, sir.'"

Yeah, thanks a lot Margaret.

I was mad, but she was right. All I had to do was be like Margaret and I could coast through life. The truth is I would have given anything to be more like my big sister. She had it all figured out—do what you're told and no one gets hurt. Unfortunately, my personality and that philosophy were like oil and water—I constantly bumped heads with Mama. But not Margaret, she just rolled with the punches and rarely got bent out of shape about anything. Even when she did get upset, it never lasted very long. Like the time we traded punches in the hall because she tripped over her own feet. I found her in our bedroom a few minutes later.

"Hey, Marg, let's go outside and jump on the trampoline."

Smiling, she said, "Okay, you can jump first."

Just like that, she was over it. No grudges, no jabs, nothing—just over it. No counseling, no medication—over it.

She still doles out advice and every once in a while, when all is right in the world and the stars are aligned, she speaks as only an older and much wiser sister could.

I was in town for a short visit and was talking to Mama about leaving my job in Miami to move closer to home. We were on our way to the mall to do some shopping. Mama and I were in the front seat and Margaret was sitting quietly in the back.

"I'm thinking about moving back to Atlanta," I said to Mama.

"Oh, honey, that would be wonderful."

"Yeah, I think it's time, but I have no idea what I'm going to do about a job. I don't know if I should leave Miami until I have something secure in Atlanta."

From the back seat came the voice of reason. "You know, Embry, it's easier to get a job if you already have a job."

Mama and I looked at each other and smiled. Did she know what she was talking about or was she just repeating something she'd heard? Surely, it had to be the latter. Either way, she was right. I needed to find a job in Atlanta before I left Florida. I realized things hadn't changed in twenty-five years. Margaret was always there when I needed her.

Square One

THE SUMMER OF 1963, MAMA NEEDED a plan. Margaret was five years old and posed a challenge—she was learning faster than Mama could teach. Soon, I would be starting preschool and Mama was thinking about going back to work. What was she going to do with Margaret?

Unsure of her options, Mama immediately ruled out the public schools. First of all, she didn't know if they'd accept Margaret and secondly, she was concerned about placing Margaret in a large classroom full of unruly children. Mama was protective, though she'd never admit it to anyone.

On the advice of a family friend, Mama decided to look into a private preschool and kindergarten at a small Baptist church that was close to our neighborhood.

Mama's always said she does better in person than on the phone, so she made an appointment with the director, a kind but serious woman named Harriet Buff.

"What did you say to her?" I asked.

"I don't really remember what I said, just that I wanted to enroll my daughter in the preschool."

"What did you tell her about Margaret?"

"Well, I told her the problem, you know."

"You mean you told her that Margaret had Down syndrome?"

"I don't remember if I said that or not."

I think this was the first time I realized how important it was to Mama that no one put a label on Margaret. She made up her mind very early on that she wasn't going to acquiesce to someone else's expectations for her child.

"Did Mrs. Buff have any reservations about admitting Margaret?"

"No, she was thrilled," Mama said. "She thought it would be wonderful for the other children to be around Margaret."

And so began Margaret's academic career. She attended the private church school for three years—two years in preschool and one year in kindergarten. Margaret didn't start preschool until she was five, so by the time she was starting her second year, I had turned four and Mama enrolled me as well. Unfortunately, I was placed in a different classroom from my sister, and even though I have no recollection of the events that transpired on that first day, Mama says it was memorable.

"You pitched a fit when you found out you weren't in Margaret's class."

"What do you mean I pitched a fit?"

"Oh, you cried and carried on because you wanted to be in the same room with Margaret."

"What did they do?"

"Well, of course they put y'all in the same class," Mama said. "They weren't about to listen to that noise every day."

I could tell Mama was nothing short of mortified by my four-year-old tantrum behavior. I don't think she realized why I wanted to be with my big sister, and the truth is, I didn't realize why either. I just knew I wanted to be close to Margaret. She had a calming effect on me. She made the experience of being in a new place with strange people not seem so scary and I needed that desperately. I clung to Mama, tentative and anxious while Margaret joined right in, no matter what the situation.

Margaret's teachers commented on her adaptability as well. They also recognized that Margaret was sweet and loving, that she drew people in like a magnet. They noticed how quickly she learned, how willing she was to help others and consequently, encouraged those unique aspects of her personality.

By the end of her kindergarten year, Margaret had accomplished the same things as every other child in her class. Her vocabulary and language skills were good, she could write her name, and most important, she was even learning to read. Margaret's teachers, along with the director of the school assured Mama that Margaret was ready for first grade. This presented a whole new dilemma: *What would Mama do now?*

Bolstered by their encouragement, Mama decided to enroll Margaret in our neighborhood school, Rigdon Road Elementary. She felt like it was the right thing to do. After all, Jake had spent six years there and done just fine. Mama made a trip to the school to meet the principal face to face and explain her situation.

"All I'm asking is that you let her try," Mama told him. "She did well in kindergarten. She's very capable."

"Well, alright," he said. "We'll let her try, but I'm not guaranteeing anything."

His attitude was dismal, but Mama felt she had no other choice. That fall, Margaret started first grade in a regular class, with regular books, regular kids and a regular teacher.

Everything went well at first, but as the weeks went by, Margaret's teacher started getting frustrated. She complained that Margaret couldn't keep up with the other children in her class and this teacher, whoever she was, didn't have the patience or the willingness to make accommodations. Finally, she gave up altogether.

"I don't want her to come back after Christmas," she told Mama. "She's too slow and I don't know what to do with her."

Mama was back to square one.

One of a Kind

THE YEAR MARGARET STARTED FIRST GRADE, there were three primary classrooms in the city of Columbus for children with special needs. Mama didn't know anything about this, though, and, evidently, neither did the principal at Margaret's school.

The teachers in those classrooms got by on little or no assistance from the state. They bought their own supplies and designed their own curriculum. They pored over long lists of children with disabilities and were forced to choose students based on sketchy background information. Doing the best with what they were given, they dedicated themselves to providing a supportive environment for children who were disabled.

In 1967, children with disabilities were labeled and placed in one of three categories: *Trainable* (children with mild to moderate intellectual impairment); *Multi-Handicap* (children with physical disabilities who may or may not have had intellectual disabilities); or *Severe and Profound* (children who were considered to be non-functioning).

Each classroom could accommodate twelve children between the ages of six and thirteen and if a child wasn't chosen to attend one of these classes, that child stayed at home.

Dee Rainey, the teacher of the "Trainable" class and a

childhood friend of Mama's, agreed to meet with me and tell me the story of how she became Margaret's first special education teacher.

Dee invited me to her house on a Sunday afternoon in February. When I came in, the first thing she asked was if I'd like to see her dog, a Jack Russell terrier named Peg. We walked to the back of her house into a large den with dark wood paneling, lots of family photographs, and comfy furniture. Adorning the walls were framed charcoal drawings of seven of her previous dogs.

I was looking at the sketches when Peg and another dog that Dee was taking care of bounded in from the back yard. Peg jumped up and down, while Dixie, the guest dog, sat quietly at Dee's feet. Dee has had many dogs in her sixty-nine years and most of them are buried in her back yard in graves marked with a personalized headstone. Dee is passionate about her dogs. She's also passionate about golf and bridge and her den is a testament to all three.

After the dogs went back outside, we sat down at a card table Dee uses for her weekly bridge game. Spread out on the table was several pictures of Margaret and her classmates: posed class pictures, eight by ten head shots, candid shots of students in scout uniforms, students with members of the local community and one picture of Margaret's class with a celebrity—Miss Georgia, 1969.

As I leafed through the photos, Dee pointed to a small notepad in the corner of the table. "Before you came over I wrote some things down so I wouldn't forget them."

Dee Rainey is the quintessential southern lady. She's classy, sporty and has beautiful manners. I notice that her accent sounds just like Mama's. Even though Dee's several years younger than Mama, I can tell they grew up during the same era.

This afternoon she's dressed in a neat pair of slacks and a turtleneck. Her silver jewelry accents her perfectly styled hair. Her personality, wit and charm seem immense for her petite stature. I'm immediately aware that I enjoy being in her company.

"So, how do you want to get started?" she asks.

"Well, I guess I'd like to know what made you want to teach special education."

"Oh well, okay. Let's see. I was teaching second grade at Edwina Wood," she said. "I guess I'd been teaching there about ten years."

She avoided eye contact with me for a minute and bowed her head. "I'm probably going to start crying when I tell you this."

I didn't know what to say, if anything, so I looked down at my paper and waited.

"It was the beginning of the school year," she continued, "and each teacher got a lunchroom assignment. Well, the first day of school, I took my class into the cafeteria as I'd done many times before and asked where we would be sitting." Dee continued to look down at the table, her hands folded tightly.

"Someone came up and told me that my class would be sitting at a different table this year, that our table would be next to the special children. Embry, I couldn't believe it. I got so mad that as soon as school was out, I marched down to the principal's office and demanded to know why my class had to sit next to 'those children.'"

"What did he say?" I asked.

"He said, 'Well, Miss Rainey, I chose your class because I thought you were a nice person and you wouldn't mind.'"

Tears welled up in her eyes. She looked away and dabbed at them with a Kleenex.

"I felt terrible," she said. "I was so embarrassed by my behavior. Soon after that, I started taking my class to play with the special children once a week. I thought it would be good for them to get to know those children and learn to be accepting of them, and it was certainly good for me.

"Later in the school year," she continued, "the teacher of the 'trainable' class got sick and asked me if I wanted to take over for her. I was nervous about it, but I knew it was an opportunity I couldn't pass up. I gave up teaching second grade, took over her class and went back to school during the summer to get my certification." She looked at me and smiled. "I taught that class for the next twenty-six years."

"I had no idea," I said. "I thought you always taught special ed."

"To tell you the truth, I feel like I did. Every day was a new experience, but I learned so much from my students. I won't ever forget any of them."

"Mama told me that you contacted her about enrolling Margaret in your class. Do you remember that?"

"I do," she said. "Margaret's name came across my desk and I thought she would be perfect for my class."

"Mama said she thought it was during the Christmas holidays."

"Yes, I believe it was. The class wasn't full, so I was able to take another student."

"Did you know that Margaret's teacher at Rigdon Road told Mama not to bring Margaret back after Christmas?"

"No, I didn't at the time."

"Pretty amazing, huh?"

"Yes, it seems like quite a coincidence," Dee said. "But I knew it wasn't a coincidence at all."

"So what was Margaret like in school?" I said.

"Margaret was one of the smartest students I ever had," Dee said. "She was so articulate and well-mannered. She could do anything, you know. Whatever I put in front of her, she would try it."

I beamed. "Mrs. Sanders said the same things about Margaret."

"Rosa Sanders?"

"Yes, ma'am, the teacher she had after you."

"I don't doubt it," Dee said. "Margaret was a fast learner. She could read and write very well. She was pretty good at math too and she could memorize anything. She always had a part in the Christmas play. I know one year she played the part of the angel Gabriel. Margaret was perfect and remembered all her lines. We were so proud."

"Do you remember this?" I showed Dee a note she had

written to Margaret, dated December 1970.

"I found it in Margaret's scrapbook." I unfolded the worn piece of paper and handed it to Dee.

She read it aloud. "'*Margaret, you're a Christmas angel, born in January. Love, Miss Rainey.*'" She looked as if she was going to cry again, but instead a smile brightened her face. "She *was* an angel," Dee said. "That Margaret's one of a kind."

Oral Recitation

AFTER SPENDING FIVE YEARS WITH DEE Rainey, Margaret and most of her classmates were transferred to Talbotton Road Junior High School, an old, run-down building in a poor section of town. The one bright spot in that school was the special education teacher, Rosa Lee Sanders.

Determined that her students would achieve success as well as recognition, Mrs. Sanders challenged them to do their best. She encouraged Margaret to discover her potential and Margaret responded with enthusiasm. By the end of her second year, Margaret had been presented with almost every award the school gave out: outstanding science student, outstanding physical education student, outstanding drama student and perfect attendance. Margaret had so many certificates from Talbotton Road Junior High that Mama had to buy a scrapbook just to hold them all.

I never had the chance to meet Mrs. Sanders, so instead of paying a personal visit, I decided to call her on the phone. After introducing myself, I said, "I know it's been a long time, but I was wondering if you could tell me something about Margaret when she was in your class."

"Well, it has been a long time, dear," she responded. "You know, I retired in 1982."

"No, ma'am, I didn't know."

"Oh yes, dear, I'm seventy-four years old," she continued. "But I remember Margaret well."

"Oh, I'm so glad," I said. "I'm writing a book about Margaret and I would love for you to share anything you can remember."

"I remember all of my students, dear," she said, letting me know right away that she was in charge of the conversation.

"Yes, ma'am," I replied.

"But, I'll tell you what I remember most about Margaret," she said, her voice becoming softer. "She was excellent at oral recitation."

I laughed. "Margaret's always been good at talking."

"Oh, I don't mean just talking, dear. Margaret was very good at memorization and her speech was so beautiful, you know. I had the class put on an Easter play every year and Margaret always had a lead role."

"I had no idea," I said, somewhat embarrassed that I didn't know anything about Margaret's acting career and sad that I never got to see my sister perform.

Mrs. Sanders crashed my pity party. "Margaret would usually play the part of Mary Magdalene," she stated. "One year, she did a pantomime of when Mary goes to the cemetery to look for Jesus. Well, as you know, dear, Jesus was not there. Margaret searched around the tomb and then, right on cue, she pretended to cry and wail just as if she'd missed Jesus herself. I mean to tell you, she really put on a show."

"I should've known that Margaret would be good at acting," I said. "She's always been good at expressing herself."

"I still remember that performance well," Mrs. Sanders said. "The principal even came up to me afterward and told me how much he liked it. Yes, Margaret got praise from everyone that day."

"I'm sure Margaret loved that," I responded. "She's never been one to step out of the spotlight."

"Oh, she loved it alright, and when the play was over, she stood up and gave her own self a clap."

About Daddy

LIKE A LOT OF MEN FROM his generation, Daddy didn't have much to do with his children. It wasn't that he didn't like us, he just didn't know what to do with us, especially me and Margaret. Besides, Daddy thought taking care of children was women's work. He wasn't to be bothered with that and Mama wasn't going to force him to get used to it.

An only child whose father died when he was in his late teens, Daddy's life revolved around his work, his hobbies and his family, but mostly his work and his hobbies. He wanted to go to college, but his mother put the squeeze on him to stay in Columbus and take care of her, so Daddy decided to become a mechanic. He worked for Mr. Hooten for several years, then chose to open his own business, a carburetor repair shop in the heart of downtown. "The shop," as he called it, is where Daddy spent most of his time.

Daddy also spent a lot of time piddling around in the garage building things or putting together model airplanes. He loved gadgets and bought every new tool that came on the market. He amused himself by sticking messages on every new item he purchased.

I snuck out to his storage room one day to find his label maker. *How cool would it be to make my own labels?* I thought. Then

Margaret would have to leave my stuff alone. I knew exactly where he kept it and waited until no one was around. As I headed back into the house, I pulled the prize out from under my shirt to get a good look at it and something caught my eye. A label stuck to the label maker that read: *Keep your syrupy hands off!*

If Daddy wasn't in the garage, he could be found indulging himself in his other passions—reading and listening to classical music. He read constantly and even though he never studied past high school, he was one of the smartest people I've ever known.

Daddy lived on pretense, which is something Mama has never done. He wore white shirts to work instead of blue ones because he didn't want to be regarded as a blue-collar worker. We never ate pasta of any kind because Daddy said that's what poor people ate. He was a staunch Republican and his heroes were people like George Wallace, former Georgia Governor Lester Maddox and Archie Bunker.

I never knew any of this growing up. Most of what I know about Daddy I've learned from Mama; not from any conversations I had with my father. He didn't have conversations with us. He had conversations about us and around us, but rarely with us.

"Your daddy was as hardheaded as they come and he was always right. Nobody could tell him anything," Mama said. "He took the head rests out of his car because he said he'd be damned if the government was going to tell him what to do."

Daddy struggled with Margaret's diagnosis, he couldn't help himself. He wanted things to be just so and went to great pains to make sure of that in his own life. He told Mama how to vote, he told her what she should and shouldn't buy, he even tried to control how she thought, but Mama was too smart for that. She just nodded and agreed. She had to keep the peace.

At times, Daddy attempted to entertain us and it seemed to me that he went all out to make Margaret laugh. He'd walk through the den when we were watching television and burp or pass gas. Without ever cracking a smile he'd say, "Whoops, stepped on a frog."

Margaret would get so tickled, she'd laugh herself into an asthma attack. Daddy was fun when he wasn't playing the part of absent father.

When we were little, he gave all of us nicknames. Margaret's was "Tooks McGooks," mine was "Mut," and for as long as I can remember, he called my big brother "Bud."

If Daddy was in a good mood, he would read to us from an old tattered copy of *Uncle Remus*. He could enunciate perfectly in the old southern dialect, which we loved. I think Daddy wanted to make us happy; he just wasn't sure how to go about it.

"So, how do you think Daddy really felt about Margaret?" I asked Mama many years after Daddy had died.

She bowed her head and was silent for a minute or two. "Your daddy didn't know how to say it, but I think he was real proud of her."

Just Like Her

NOT LONG AFTER I STARTED WRITING, I read one of my stories to Mama. When I finished, we sat across from each other, the room filled with heavy silence.

"Well, what do you think?"

"Dear Father," she replied, "I think I sound like an ogre," which in Mama's thick southern accent and slow delivery sounded more like, "Deeya Fathuh, I think I sound like an oguh."

"Nobody's gonna' think you're an ogre, Mama. They'll just realize what a strong, independent woman you are, and that you let people know where they stand."

"Humph."

"Well, look at it this way, Mama. At least they'll know you take your job as a parent seriously."

She gave me a stern look. "If I hadn't made sure Margaret knew right from wrong, there's no telling what would've happened to her. I had to be tough on her. She was my responsibility you know, not anybody else's."

My mother's strength and fortitude came with her upbringing. Born in 1919 in the mill town of Columbus, Georgia, Mama grew up during the Depression. Augusta Embry Andrews was named for her grandfather, George Augustus Pearce, and her grandmother, Ida Melissa Embry. She was the oldest of four girls.

When her first sister was born, Mama was four years old and she immediately assumed the role of caretaker. Their mother was strict and she expected her oldest daughter to set a good example for her younger siblings. The Andrews family suffered through the Depression and then even greater tragedy when Mabel, the youngest of the four girls died of pneumonia. Mama learned quickly how to take care of herself as well as those around her.

Mama was very close to her father, who was known to all of his grandchildren as "Papa." Papa raised Jersey cows and ran a dairy farm just across the Chattahoochee River from their home in downtown Columbus. A parking lot now sits in place of the once beautiful Victorian home Mama grew up in; the result of renovations to the historic downtown area.

When Mama was young, she loved going to the farm with Papa. She spent her time riding horses, milking cows and learning about life. She cherished her time with him and people have always said that the two of them were like peas and carrots.

Papa was a strong, quiet man who was well respected in the community. Mama looked up to him and wanted so much to please him.

"Papa always said I was his only son," Mama joked. "So, I just learned how to do everything he did."

And Mama's right, she could do anything a man could do, from planting a garden to tarring a roof, as well as anything that women in her day were expected to do, from sewing her own clothes to baking a cake. There's nothing that Mama can't do.

Many years ago, I received a letter from my Aunt Isabel, the oldest of Mama's sisters. I was surprised, maybe even shocked by what she had to say about Mama—mainly because my mother and her sisters are a dying breed; a generation of women who don't discuss emotional issues with anyone, even their own family. At the same time, you will never hear them fret or complain. They just put their heads down and plow through, no matter what the circumstance.

I was also shocked by my aunt's admission of how much she had looked up to Mama. I had no idea the influence my mother had on her siblings. Isabel told me that she had always admired Mama for her strength and perseverance. In so many words, she said that Mama had set the bar so high, neither of her sisters could ever walk in her shoes.

Stirred by her candor, I realized what an inspiration my mother was to me and that I had never felt prouder to be her daughter.

I thought back to the day Mama and I went to see our old housekeeper Katie Mae Baker just a few years before she died. I was in my early twenties and hadn't seen Katie since I was four years old. As we walked up the front steps, Katie met us at the door. She smiled her beautiful smile and said, "Oooh, Miss Gusta, she's just like you."

Her words touched me deeply, even though I knew that Katie was just referring to how much I looked like Mama. I think about that now though and can only hope that one day those words will mean so much more.

Competitor

As THE INFANTRY BAND AND COLOR guard marched around the track, horns blazing and flags flying, dozens of special athletes fell in behind, smiling and waving at cheering fans. The year was 1970, the event, my sister's first Special Olympics, a spring track meet in our hometown of Columbus, Georgia. Margaret was just thirteen years old.

The coaches had signed Margaret up for several events that day. Even though they had only been working with her a short time, they knew she was one of the best athletes our town had to offer.

The day of the meet, Margaret had to be at the track at 8:00 a.m. Usually, getting her out of bed before 9:00 is like pulling teeth, but that wasn't that case when it came to Special Olympics. Somehow, Margaret understood the significance of this day—she was up and ready to go at seven.

Margaret's first event was the broad jump, then the softball throw, and last, but certainly not least, the fifty yard dash.

She medalled in her first two events and then, as the afternoon sun was setting, the call came for participants in the fifty yard dash, the race she had looked forward to all day.

Margaret was in a heat with four other runners. When the gun sounded, all five of them took off for the finish line. Four of them, including Margaret, laughed the whole way down the track. The only one who wasn't laughing won the race. As they crossed the finish line, their designated "hugger" came up and greeted each one.

One of the most wonderful things about Special Olympics is the volunteers whose only job is to hug each athlete at the completion of their event. If you've never experienced Special Olympics, you should treat yourself at least once—you will forever be affected. These athletes give everything they have for the sheer joy of participating. To this day, I don't make it through one event without being overcome with tears of joy.

Following her race, Margaret was called to the podium for the medal ceremony. As they pinned the fourth place ribbon to her shirt, you could see a new determination in her eyes. From that moment forward, she was a woman transformed. She had tasted competition and she did *not* like losing. Margaret's competitive spirit was about to surface.

Fast-forward a few years. This time, I volunteered to be a hugger for the track events. Margaret and I were talking the night before the meet.

"I'm gonna win first place," she said to me during supper.

"In what?" I casually responded.

"Everything," she said, shrugging her shoulders.

Gone was the happy-go-lucky attitude of the past. Here today was Margaret, the competitor.

Once again, the fifty yard dash was her last event of the day. The field of six waited at the start line. Margaret was crouched in a runner's stance, her face the picture of concentration. All of a sudden, they were off and two runners quickly jumped ahead of Margaret. She was fast, but they were faster. As hard as she tried, she couldn't make up the deficit. Third place was the best she could do.

I went to congratulate and hug my assigned athlete and watched Margaret out of the corner of my eye.

"Congratulations, you came in third place," Margaret's hugger said.

As I put my arm around the young woman who had won the race, I noticed Margaret shaking her head and saying something to her hugger. I could tell the young volunteer didn't quite know how to handle the situation. I started pushing my way through the crowd to where they were standing.

Once I was closer I knew what the fuss was all about.

"I didn't get third place," Margaret said loudly, "I got first place."

I touched Margaret on the shoulder and said, "You need to do what she says, Margaret, and take the third place medal."

"Embry, I don't want third place. I want first place!"

"You didn't win first place, Margaret."

"Yes, I did!" she countered.

"Margaret, did you see those two people who crossed the finish line in front of you?"

"Yes, I did."

"Well, if two people were in front of you, you didn't come in first place."

She stood there for a minute not saying anything. Margaret's terrible at math, but I knew even she could put this one together. She looked at me and then at her hugger and realized the argument was futile. She turned and walked to the awards stand to receive her medal.

As she stepped down from the podium, I put my arm around her and gave her my best sisterly advice.

"You better not pull another stunt like that one again, Margaret. Do you know what Mama would do if she found out?"

"Yes, I do," she said.

"What?"

"She probably wouldn't let me come back."

"Well," I said, "do you want that to happen?"

She looked at me as if I'd just asked the dumbest question known to man. "Embry, I'm not gonna tell Mama."

Pushing the Envelope

MARGARET AND I DID ALMOST EVERYTHING together when we were little. We took dancing lessons and swimming lessons together. We took ceramics and music lessons together. When I started horseback riding, Margaret probably would have done that too, if it hadn't been for the bad experience she had the first day at the stables.

It was my sixth birthday and I was on top of the world. Mama, Daddy, Margaret and I all loaded up in the car to drive over to Alabama, where I would take my first riding lesson. As soon as we got to the barn, I jumped out and ran over to the first horse I saw. Margaret, a little more tentative, stood next to the car with Daddy. After a few minutes, she decided it was safe to explore her surroundings and set off toward the barn.

Her first encounter was an old, decrepit horse affectionately known as Nell. A barnyard pet, Nell was allowed to wander around freely, untethered and unsupervised. I guess Margaret could sense that Nell was harmless so she walked over to pet her. In an attempt to get as close as she could to her admirer, Nell stepped on Margaret's foot, and even a hysterical child can't budge a deaf and blind horse.

Needless to say, it took several minutes and several people to get Nell off Margaret's foot. Many years would pass before

Margaret was comfortable around horses.

Margaret loved dancing lessons and swimming lessons, and was really good at both. I absolutely despised the dancing lessons —mostly because I was terrible at it, but also because it was just too girly for me. Falling off horses was much more fun.

Mama let me quit dancing, but we had to complete all of our swimming classes. You see Mama was an excellent swimmer, and had at one time been an aquatics director for the Girl Scouts. She was determined that her children would learn to swim.

From the first time she ever stepped into a pool, Margaret was a natural. She was never afraid of the water, and breezed through her swimming lessons. This would eventually pay off in her adulthood, as she won many medals in swimming competitions in the Special Olympics.

I remember one meet in particular when Margaret was about twelve or thirteen, a preliminary for the state competition. We were all excited—Margaret had proven to us she was a great swimmer—now, all she had to do was prove it to the rest of the world.

Mama, Daddy and I were in the stands, and when the gun went off, everyone dove in, except Margaret. Swinging her arms like a mad woman, she stood glued to the side of the pool.

Finally, Mama yelled from the stands, "Margaret, what's the matter?"

Shivering, Margaret replied, "It's too cold!"

Mama didn't have much patience for this kind of thing. "Dive in anyway!" she shouted.

Margaret finally jumped in after everyone else was about halfway down the pool. She was such a good swimmer that even after starting at least twenty seconds behind the field, she still came in third place! Off to the state games she went.

In 1992, Margaret qualified again for state competition, which meant a trip to Atlanta and Emory University. I was living in Miami at the time, and decided to fly to Atlanta to surprise her.

When I got to the pool, I walked through the stands looking for the group from Columbus. Someone spotted me and told me where they were sitting. I found Margaret and snuck up behind her.

"Hey, Marg," I said, in my most jovial voice.

Margaret turned around and stared at me, completely startled and confused. All of a sudden, she jumped up, threw her arms around me and started crying. Then, I started crying—so we just stood there, hugging and crying.

Mama met me there later and we found a seat in the stands. We both remarked how Margaret had a really good chance to win her heat, as long as she didn't pull another stunt like the one years ago. We talked about that and had a good laugh, but what Mama was most worried about today was what Margaret would do if she *did* win the race. Apparently, when she won her qualifying heat, some excessive celebration had taken place.

"I told Margaret not to do all that putting her arms up in the air like those people do on television," Mama said. "I told her to just take her medal and say thank you."

"What do you mean?" I asked.

"She sees all those athletes on TV dancing around and acting the fool. I told her not to do that."

As fate would have it, Margaret won the race. Mama was sitting on pins and needles during the medal ceremony. She was very proud and happy that Margaret had won, but she was more worried about what was about to happen. After they put the medal around her neck, Margaret rose up and began pumping her fists in the air. She couldn't help herself. She was basking in the moment, and like all great athletes, she had to celebrate!

Well, that was just too much. It may have even been "common." That's what Mama calls anything she deems unladylike. It's common.

After telling that story many times, a couple of my friends began referring to that move as "the Margaret." They told me that while on a ski trip in Colorado, they went down a really difficult run. When they got to the bottom, obviously relieved and exhilarated, they looked at each other, pumped their fists in the air and did "the Margaret"!

61

After the race was over, Mama and I went to congratulate Margaret. I knew I had to be the buffer, so I ran up and gave her a big hug.

"Way to go, Margaret—that's awesome!"

Mama was only a couple of steps behind me. I kept my arm around Margaret and braced myself.

"Now, Margaret, I told you not to do that," Mama announced.

Margaret knew exactly what Mama was talking about. "Mama, that's what you're supposed to do!"

"Well, don't do it again!"

"Ugh, Mama!!" Margaret whined.

"I'm real proud of you, but I told you to just take your medal and say thank you."

"Mama, I did say thank you!"

Margaret won another race that day; however, the celebration was toned down a bit. After years of living with Mama, Margaret knows just how far she can push the envelope.

Lawn Mowers

WHEN MARGARET WAS SEVENTEEN AND I was fifteen, Mama and Daddy decided that we should uproot ourselves and move to the country. For years, they talked about buying a few acres of land and building a house on it, but complained that taxes were too high in Georgia.

Determined not to let dreams die, my parents set their sights across the river. Their families had lived in Georgia for oh, around 200 years, and just like that—identity crisis—we were moving to Alabama.

Daddy found six acres of beautiful rolling hills just across the Chattahoochee River in Alabama, but even though we had moved to a new state, we clung to the old one. As the crow flies, our new house was only about eleven miles from the Columbus city limits, or "town" as the country folks called it. We clocked it one day— twenty minutes to civilization. That was important, we might need to get to town in a hurry.

I wasn't very happy about the move, but then again, no one asked for my opinion. They attempted to smooth things over by using my horse as leverage.

"You'll be able to keep Champ right in the back yard," Mama said. "We'll build a barn and everything."

I was still opposed, but the horse thing was making me soft.

Margaret didn't care, as long as she had a television, she was happy.

Thank goodness we lived right on the highway. Life could've been boring in Seale, Alabama, population 502, if not for the traffic. All we had to do was get out in the yard and do something, anything, and folks driving by would honk and wave. It was a really good honking day if I was riding my horse in the front yard. I did that at least once a week—my gift to all those weary travelers.

Our neighbors were no less exciting than all the traffic on the highway. About a year after we arrived, a family with about five or six kids moved in across the road. I say "about" because there were so many coming and going, we never knew exactly who belonged and who didn't.

Once a week, the oldest boy would stomp through our yard and into our pasture with a shotgun slung over his shoulder. A few hours later, he'd stomp back through with a bag full of rabbits, squirrels and various other vermin.

This family didn't know borders or boundaries of any kind. They'd come into our yard and jump on our trampoline or start shooting at our basketball goal completely uninvited. It was creepy.

One summer day, we heard a knock at the door. I peeked out the window to see the youngest girl, Tootsie, who couldn't have been more than six or seven, standing on the front porch.

Mama was already headed to the door, so I joined her. She opened it to find this skinny, dirty little girl smiling up at her with a huge dip of snuff in her bottom lip.

"Yes, can I help you?" Mama said, forcing a smile.

Tootsie flashed a snuff stained grin. "My mommer wants to know if she can borry some vin-A-ger," she announced.

"I beg your pardon?" Mama said, shaking her head.

She got louder. "My mommer needs some vin-A-ger!"

We couldn't figure out if Tootsie's ability to communicate was more impaired by the snuff in her mouth, the hillbilly accent, or her cognitive functioning. She wanted vinegar, which finally came to us after ten minutes of her screaming and Mama and I looking at each other saying, "Borry some what?"

For the most part, they seemed rather harmless, albeit somewhat rough around the edges, until they let our dog out of the fence, tossed a huge rock through my bedroom window and broke into our house. They gave themselves away when two of the boys started fighting over who was the best rock thrower.

A few months later they moved away and life went back to normal, well, semi-normal.

Bubba Smiley lived at the top of the hill. He decided he wanted to court me, so he rode down the hill one day on a riding lawn mower and hung around all afternoon.

Now Bubba didn't have bat brains as Mama would say, and he smelled. He was real sweet, just not the kind of boy you wanted getting very close to you. I kept hoping something would happen to that lawn mower—what I didn't know is that his daddy worked on lawn mowers and had about 150 of them in front of their house. A lawn mower malfunction wasn't going to save me from anything.

When we were teenagers, Mama never pushed us into socializing, especially with boys, but for some reason, she felt sorry for Bubba.

"Bubba's driving me crazy," I said to no one in particular at supper one night.

Mama shook her head. "He's just right pitiful, isn't he?"

"Yes, he is and I feel sorry for him, but he wants me to be his girlfriend and I don't wanna get involved with him like that."

"You don't have to get involved with him, just be friendly to him."

No sooner had she gotten the words out of her mouth, than Bubba began to ride down the hill five times a week. After a couple of weeks of this, I didn't care what Mama said, something had to be done. So, I told him I had a boyfriend, which I didn't, but anyway, it worked. He started courting Margaret.

Other than his grandmother, Margaret was the only person in a fifty-mile radius of that small town that would pay attention to Bubba.

Margaret doesn't discriminate based on brains, smell or any other attributes the rest of us deem necessary in a mate. Not to mention, she enjoyed the company. Bubba would spend hours with her listening to records, watching TV or playing games. Margaret didn't want a mate, she had Jonathan. He was her real boyfriend, but nothing was ever said about him. That wasn't necessary. Margaret didn't know Bubba was courting and Bubba didn't know he may as well have been a toad that could sing, dance and play Parcheesi.

After a few months of Bubba and Margaret, his visits waned. We wondered, but didn't dare ask. Then, his grandmother called one day to tell Mama that Bubba had found a girlfriend. A nice girl he met at church. We later found out that he got her pregnant, twice.

I waited, but Mama didn't say anything. I wondered why she had reserved comment for so long. Then, I realized she had been trying to figure out the best way to save face.

"So, Mama, what do you think about Bubba and his new girlfriend?" I asked.

"Well, I guess it's good that he found somebody, although I can't imagine who'd want him. Thank goodness I raised the two of you with enough sense not to get involved with him."

I shook my head. "Yeah, thank goodness for that."

Smoking

AFTER GRADUATING FROM HIGH SCHOOL, I was off to college. After Margaret graduated from high school, she went to boot camp. At least that's what it seemed like to me. Actually, it was a vocational rehabilitation facility in Montgomery, Alabama. A place designed to help people with disabilities learn independent daily living skills as well as some basic job skills. But, just like boot camp, she had to stay there for six weeks without coming home. Well, for Margaret that was fine, but for me and Mama, it was traumatic.

The three of us left on a Sunday afternoon and drove to Montgomery. Daddy was really sick at the time, so he stayed at home. When we arrived, the first thing we noticed were people wandering aimlessly around the building. This made Mama and me ill at ease. I immediately thought of *One Flew Over the Cuckoo's Nest.* We looked at each other, and were thinking exactly the same thing. Margaret doesn't belong in a place like this!

Our guides took us on a tour of the facility, including several work areas and Margaret's new living quarters. We were introduced to several people and someone talked about all the wonderful things she would be doing while she was there. It was all a blur and I felt a lump rise in my throat as the smiling employee droned on and on.

Margaret, however, was perfectly content, maybe even excited about her new adventure. She put her bags down, sat on her new bed and bounced up and down a few times.

"Look, Embry, it's real comfortable."

"That's great, Marg. This is a nice room," I said, fighting back tears.

Reluctantly, and after several instructions from Mama, we left. I was going to school at Auburn University at the time, so Mama dropped me off on the way home. I cried for most of the trip back while Mama remained calm and collected. "Well, I'm sure she'll be fine," was all she said. Mama was worried, but she would never let it show.

Even though Margaret wasn't allowed to come home for six weeks, she was allowed to have visitors. Since I was only fifty miles down the road from her in Auburn, I talked one of my roommates into going with me one Sunday to pay a visit.

When we walked in, several people, once again wandering aimlessly around, came up and started talking to us. My friend was scared to death and wanted to wait in the car. I made her stay, and finally we found Margaret. I had worried that she would be homesick, but she was fine. She had made friends with everyone and was now the center's most popular resident. Give Margaret a lemon and she'll make a pitcher of lemonade.

When the time came for Margaret's first visit home, Mama arranged for a Greyhound bus to pick her up in Montgomery, bring her home and then take her back to the center again on Sunday. Margaret was thrilled with riding the bus. Well, unbeknownst to any of us, the thrills were just beginning.

Not only had Margaret gained several pounds, but she had stashed away three packs of *Kool* cigarettes in her purse. Margaret has an affinity for vending machines. She likes putting money in and watching something come out, it doesn't really matter what it is. She had seen several people at her center buying cigarettes, so she thought she'd give it a try. Mama was not happy with this turn of events.

"Now, Margaret, why on earth would you buy cigarettes?"

68

"Mama, lots of people were buying them."

I was waiting for—*If so and so jumped in the river, would you jump too?*—but it never came. Mama didn't waste time with conjecture; she got right to the point. "Margaret, you better not be smoking cigarettes, and you certainly better not put any more of your money into those damn machines!"

The cigarettes went in the trash can and Margaret went back to Montgomery on the Greyhound bus on Sunday.

During one of Margaret's subsequent visits, I came home to find no one in the house. At least that's what I thought, until I noticed that Margaret's bedroom door was closed. This was very odd—no one in our house ever closed our bedroom doors.

"Margaret, what are you doing in there?" I said.

"Nothing."

"Why do you have the door closed?"

I opened it and found her standing behind the door with her arm behind her back and smoke billowing around her head.

"Margaret, are you smoking?"

Shaking her head, she said, "No."

Margaret has always been clueless about hiding. When we played hide-and-seek as kids, she would put her head under a table or a chair and leave her entire body sticking out with her butt straight up in the air. Some things never change.

I couldn't resist a test, though, to see if she really knew what she was doing. "Let me see you smoke that cigarette."

She took a drag, inhaled, and blew smoke out of her nose! As impressed as I was, I told her she was going to have to get rid of the cigarettes, so I just took them. I was a young college coed—I had done a little cigarette smoking myself.

Now, if Margaret hears anyone say anything about smoking, or trying to quit smoking, she feels compelled to join the conversation.

"I don't smoke any more," she says. "I quit."

Salvation

DADDY DIED IN FEBRUARY 1983. WHAT I remember most vividly was the phone call that came at six o'clock in the morning. When you're in college, nobody calls that early unless something is terribly wrong. This day was no exception.

The sound of the phone jolted me out of a deep sleep. My roommates, who were night owls and oblivious to anything that happened before nine o'clock, slept soundly in the next room. I stumbled through the darkness into the kitchen and grabbed the phone on the fourth or fifth ring.

"Hello?" I said, praying it wasn't for me, and at the same time, praying that it wasn't bad news for either one of my roommates.

"Embry?" My mother's voice was soft, almost a whisper, angelic.

Panic swept over me. *Something has happened to Margaret*, I thought. "What's wrong, Mama?" I blurted into the silence.

Mama didn't respond right away, but when she did, her voice was calm, composed. She wasn't crying or choked up at all. She was very matter of fact, as if she had called to pass on some uninteresting news.

"You need to come home, honey," she said. "Your daddy died last night."

I don't remember what was said after that. I slid down the wall and fell into a heap on the floor—unable to think, unable to talk, unable to do anything but cry.

Daddy got sick while I was still in high school, less than two years after we moved to the country. Nobody knew what was wrong with him, not even the doctors. Cataracts and detached retinas on both eyes had forced him into an early retirement. His vision had become so poor he could no longer perform the intricate work of rebuilding a carburetor. Daddy's work was his life and life, as he knew it, was over.

Unable to work or drive, and barely able to read, Daddy spiraled into a deep, dark hopelessness. By the time I was a freshman in college, he had started spending long hours in bed and complaining of phantom pains throughout his body. Things only got worse when he couldn't find a doctor to concur or explain any of his maladies. The only way he would leave the house was if Mama agreed to take him to another doctor, someone to tell him he wasn't crazy, that the pain wasn't just in his head. His days became consumed with proving to Mama and his doctors that he was gravely ill. He yelled, he slammed doors, he railed against God, he even threatened to kill himself.

When I came home on the weekends, he'd greet me, then retreat to his bed where he smoked incessantly and stared blankly at the television. Every couple of hours, he wandered between his bedroom and the kitchen moaning loud enough for everyone in the house to hear him. I soon realized I was frightened by him, and couldn't bear to see my once strong, confident father in such a pathetic state. I came home less and less, unable to admit to anyone, including myself, why I avoided my parents' house. Feelings of guilt and shame plagued me constantly, yet I felt powerless to overcome them. Instead, I drowned myself in whatever rebellion I could find.

Throughout all this turmoil, Mama remained steadfast. She never told anyone what went on behind their closed doors, not even me or Jake. She supported Daddy the only way she knew how—she did whatever he asked and tried to keep the peace. During this difficult time, I believe that Margaret was Mama's salvation. Her inability to understand or talk about what was happening was a blessing in disguise. As long as she had Margaret to take care of, Mama could pretend that life was normal.

Finally, in the summer of 1982, the doctors agreed that shock therapy was the only cure for Daddy. He went into the hospital for four weeks and when he came out, he was a different person. His six-foot-five-inch frame had shrunk from 210 pounds to 175. Although his body was think and frail, his spirit was young again. He laughed and joked with us, the pain that had ruled his life inexplicably vanished. He and Mama would go out to eat or go for rides in the country. That December, he joined the rest of the family at my aunt's house for Christmas dinner. If not physically, at least emotionally, Daddy seemed to be himself once again.

By January, though, his mood began to change. The pain had returned and he was beginning to have trouble breathing. Ever since he had a heart attack at age fifty-two, Daddy's doctors had warned him of the dangers of smoking, all to no avail. If anyone mentioned his health, Daddy didn't hesitate to voice his opinion. "I'll be damned if I'm gonna let those doctors take away one of the few pleasures I have left."

Within weeks, he was hospitalized and diagnosed with congestive heart failure. And just as quickly it seemed, as he had recovered, Daddy was gone. Years later, Mama would share with me a journal she kept during Daddy's illness. The last entry on February 8, 1983, read simply: *Died quietly in his sleep.*

By the time I got home that cold February day, Mama had made all the funeral arrangements and cleaned the house. She greeted me at the door and put her arms around me. I sobbed into her chest while she patted me gently on the back.

"It's alright, dahlin'," she said. "Your daddy's in a much better place now." Then, with a finality equal to that of my father's passing, she gently released me and straightened herself. "You need to go wash your face, there'll be people coming over soon."

To this day, I'm not sure why I cried so over my daddy's death. Maybe I cried because my heart carried the weight of his sadness, because on some level, I understood his soul's longing for a more fulfilled life. Maybe I cried for Margaret or Jake, or maybe I cried for Mama, my tears replacing all the ones she couldn't or wouldn't cry for her husband of forty years. Whatever the reason, I cried until my heart felt empty.

As it turns out, Margaret was my salvation as well. She let me know that she understood the meaning of my tears and would share the burden of the death of our father. Several days after the funeral, she walked into the bathroom and found me on the floor, crying. She put her arms around me and comforted me as only she could. "It's okay, Embry," she said, "I miss Daddy too."

Celebrity Bowling

IN 1987, MARGARET WAS ONE OF ninety athletes from Georgia chosen to compete in the Special Olympics World Games at the University of Notre Dame. Even though swimming and track and field had been her strong events for many years, this time she qualified in bowling.

In the mid-1980s, a woman named Loretta Flowers, who worked for the parks and recreation department, went to one of the local bowling alleys and asked if members of the therapeutic recreation program could join the bowling league. After less than a year of practicing only once a week, Margaret was hooked and bowling became her life.

She had to have the bowling ball, the bowling shoes, and the bowling bag, even the bowling shirt.

Margaret talked about bowling constantly. She wanted to go at night. She wanted to go on the weekends. She'd ask me or Mama or Jake to take her bowling. If someone came to visit, she'd ask them. Finally, I gave in and said, "Okay, let's go." I thought it would be entertaining, not to mention, I wanted to see just how good she really was.

It was fun at first. I scored 100 and she scored 100. The next week, I scored 100 and she scored 120. After I bowled 100 and she bowled 145, I gave up. I told her she should just stick with her group. I wasn't much of a challenge.

In little more than a year, Margaret had qualified to participate on an international level in a sport she only practiced once a week.

So in June of 1987, Margaret, along with the other athletes from Georgia, was treated to a weeklong stay in South Bend, Indiana. They flew on a chartered plane and were treated like royalty. Mama and Jake drove to South Bend to cheer Margaret on as well as bask in the whole Special Olympics experience. Margaret was right on her game and brought home a bronze medal. I was devastated to miss it, but I had just started a new job and wasn't able to make the trip.

I met them at the airport in Atlanta when they returned, all ninety of the Georgia athletes decked out in their red and white Special Olympics warmup suits and wearing their medals.

I burst into tears when I saw Margaret walk off the plane, and as we hugged each other, she started crying too. Jake was there snapping photos, and Mama just stood there smiling, proud, but not showing any emotion—vintage Mama.

When Margaret got back to Columbus, she was a celebrity. Her picture was in the paper and she and another athlete from Columbus, Charles Houston, were invited to appear on a local television talk show called *Good Day*. The day before Margaret's fifteen minutes of fame, Mama started in.

"Now, Margaret, don't you talk about yourself the whole time," Mama instructed in her genteel southern accent.

"Mama, I'm not," Margaret answered. "I'm gonna talk about my medal."

"Well, make sure you listen to the questions he asks you," Mama continued. "Don't just start talking about nothing."

"Mama, I can't talk about nothing."

Margaret got dressed in her Special Olympics outfit, put on her medal and waited for Mama to chauffeur her to the TV station. When they arrived, Chuck Leonard, the show's host, greeted Margaret as if she was a long-lost friend. She had met him before at some community event and of course he remembered her—no one ever forgets Margaret.

Chuck explained that he would introduce them and then ask each one a few questions about the Games. Margaret and Charles sat down and the interview began.

The first question was directed to Margaret. "What was the best part of the Special Olympics?" Chuck asked.

Margaret answered, "Eating."

Mama cringed. Margaret remembers any place or event in her life by what she had to eat. It was killing Mama that she had left that out of the pre-interview speech.

Chuck asked Charles some questions, then came back to Margaret, who sat staring at her medal. His question interrupted her silent meditation. "So, Margaret, I heard there were lots of celebrities there."

"Yes, there were," Margaret responded.

Excitedly, he said, "Oh, well who did you see?"

Margaret, still lost in the admiration of her shiny new necklace, casually pointed to the young man sitting next to her and said, "Well, Charles Houston was there."

Dial 911

MARGARET GETS HER ATHLETIC PROWESS FROM Mama. An excellent athlete when she was young, Mama graduated from Shorter College, an all-girls school in Rome, Georgia. Mama says it was mostly a "finishing" school but the only thing she ever finished was a nap. She majored in history and excelled in sports. Tennis was her favorite.

Although Mama hadn't played tennis since her college days, for some reason, when she was seventy-two, she decided to start playing again. She joined the senior league and every week as she headed out the door to a match, she'd leave with the same au revoir: "Well, I'm off to play with those old ladies."

Most of those old ladies were at least ten years her junior and none of them could hold a candle to her athletic ability. Mama kicked butt on a regular basis.

Just as she was starting to enjoy competitive tennis, Mama was diagnosed with breast cancer—she was seventy-five. After a biopsy revealed a malignant tumor, her doctor, a longtime family friend, performed a modified mastectomy, and even though her lymph nodes were spared, the doctor informed us that her tennis playing days were probably over. He was serious and concerned —he gave orders.

"Your mother's going to be real weak and she won't be able

to use her right arm for several days. Somebody's going to have to help her do everything. Will somebody be staying with her?" he said, looking right at me.

"I'll be staying with her for a few days," I said. "And of course Margaret will be there. She's a great nurse and she can handle anything Mama doles out, right, Marg?"

I put my arm around Margaret and gave her a squeeze.

He looked at Margaret and smiled. "Okay then, she's your patient now."

This doctor's longtime knowledge of our family did not make him privy to the ways of my mama. He thought he was dealing with your everyday run-of-the-mill seventy-five-year-old woman. He was not.

Within a week of coming home from the hospital, Mama was making him look like a fool. I walked into her room and found her sitting on the bed doing calisthenics.

"I don't know why they said I wouldn't be able to do this," she said, moving her right arm up and down like she was trying out a new shoulder joint.

I bristled. "Mama, are you sure you should be doing that?"

"I'm doing it, aren't I?"

Six weeks later, she was back on the tennis court beatin' up on those old ladies.

Breast cancer was a shock—her recovery from it not surprising. My mama is one of the healthiest people I know. So when she was diagnosed with congestive heart failure three years later, no one could believe it. Daddy, understandable. Mama, unbelievable.

Daddy was probably the unhealthiest person I've ever known. He smoked up to two packs of cigarettes a day and ate whatever he damn well pleased. The only exercise he ever got was walking through the house slamming doors.

Daddy's illness was long and drawn out but with Mama, everything happened fast. She was playing tennis one week and in the hospital the next. Months later, she had lost fifteen pounds, gained a pacemaker, and had a lunch date with ten pills a day. For the first time in her life, Mama looked old.

Worried that something catastrophic might happen to Mama, I decided that Margaret could use some coaching on emergency procedures. When I got to the house, I found Margaret at the computer, playing solitaire. I was serious and concerned. Now I was giving the orders.

"Margaret, I need to talk to you about Mama. I need to make sure you know what to do if something happens to her. Come in here so we can talk and you're not staring at that computer."

We sat down on the couch in the den. I turned the blaring TV down and turned to face her.

"I want you to pay attention because this is really important."

"I'm paying attention," she said.

"If something happens to Mama, all you have to do is pick up the phone and dial nine-one-one."

She interrupted me. "I know, Embry. I've seen it on TV."

"Then, you tell them your name and address and make sure you tell them what's wrong with Mama."

She was listening, but I could tell she was just being polite. I forged ahead.

"If Mama falls down or passes out—you know, if you can't wake her up, you tell them that okay?"

"Okay," she said, staring at the television.

"If she says she can't breathe or her chest hurts, if she's having trouble walking or talking, you call nine-one-one and tell them exactly what's wrong.

"Embry, I will," she said emphatically.

The phone rang and she was up in a flash to answer it.

"Oh yeah, and make sure you tell them she has a pacemaker," I said.

"Embry, I know," she called over her shoulder.

I kept telling myself, *You're only forty-five minutes away. If something happens, you can get there in a hurry.*

About a week later I called to check on them. Margaret answered the phone.

"Hey, Marg."

"Oh, hey, Embry."

"How's Mama?"

"She's fine."

"What's she doing?" I asked. "Can I talk to her?"

"She's outside raking leaves," Margaret answered.

"Raking leaves?!" I said in a panic. "Margaret, do you remember what I told you to do if something happens to Mama?"

"Yes, I do."

"What?"

"I call nine-one-one."

"And what are you supposed to tell them?"

"Um...well...I say I have a patient here who needs some help."

Thank goodness I'd gotten that trip home down to thirty-eight minutes.

Rocks

"YOU'RE GOING TO BE HOME FOR Christmas, aren't you?"

Margaret asks me the same question every year even though I've never been away from home at Christmas.

"I wouldn't be anywhere else," I reply as I launch into a loud and somewhat off-key rendition of "I'll be Home for Christmas."

"That song always reminds me of Mabel," Mama says softly to no one in particular. Margaret and I are the only ones in the room, but Mama's not looking at either one of us.

"Why?" I ask.

"She was singing it in the hospital before she died, or so I'm told."

Mama rarely talks about Mabel, no one in her family does for that matter. All I knew was that she had died of pneumonia at a young age. I waited for Mama to go on so I could learn more about the aunt I never knew.

"It was a few weeks before Christmas and Mabel was really sick. Your daddy and I were living in Aberdeen, Maryland. That's where your daddy was stationed. Somebody called," she continued. "I don't even remember who it was, and told us we better come home. Your daddy had to go to the Red Cross to get permission to leave."

"Why did he have to go to the Red Cross?"

"I'm not sure, that's just what the Army made you do back then."

"Was Mabel getting worse?" I said. "I mean, what was happening, why did they tell you to come home?"

"I think they knew she was going to die," Mama said.

She stared at the television, no emotion on her face. Mama would never admit how difficult Mabel's death was, to her, or her family.

"I just can't imagine how hard that must have been," I replied.

Mama continued to stare at the television, not saying a word. *My mother, the rock. How can she talk about this without showing any emotion?* She was the oldest, though, she had to be strong. The big sister had to hold it together for everybody else. Besides, she was married and living away from home. She was the grown-up and Mabel, she was the baby of the family; just a child, only thirteen years old.

"I can't believe she died of pneumonia."

"Well, Penicillin had just been discovered, honey. Mabel was the first person in Columbus to get it, but it was just too late."

"To think that she died right before Christmas," I added. "That's just so hard. I don't know how you get through something like that."

I wanted Mama to talk about Mabel's death. I wanted to know how she felt and if she turned to anyone for comfort. Did she lean on Daddy or did she and her sisters comfort each other? I wanted to know that my mother allowed herself to grieve over losing her baby sister; that she didn't feel she had to act as if nothing had happened, like she did when Daddy died. Not once did she shed a tear, at least not when anyone was watching.

Then, she spoke and I knew I'd never find out how she or anyone else truly felt about losing Mabel. It was also apparent how she had coped with everything in her life that was difficult, including a child with Down syndrome.

"We just had to go on living, honey. That's all you can ever do, just accept it. What other choice do you have?"

Hooked on Phonics

CHRISTMAS HAS ALWAYS BEEN FUN AT our house because of Margaret. Since she was old enough to read and write, she's made a Christmas list. When we were little, we'd go through the Sears catalog and pick out what we wanted Santa Claus to bring. As each year went by, Margaret's list got longer and longer. Soon, it became bigger than all of us and took on a life of its own.

I have lots of friends who know of the famed list and request a copy every year. Now, there's a waiting list for "The Christmas List."

For years, Margaret would thumb through the toy section and write down something from almost every page. Her list would be four or five pages long; so long, Mama had to start proofreading it.

"Now, Margaret, you've got entirely too many things on that list."

That didn't faze Margaret—she just kept on listing. As we got older, and the Sears catalog disappeared, she had to become more creative. That's when Margaret's lists got really good. The funny thing now is not what she puts on the list, but how she spells it, starting with the title, "Christmas List."

Margaret has a fascination with all things shiny. About ten years ago, a friend of mine gave her a sequin purse. It was the gaudiest thing I'd ever seen, but she loved it. After that, she started adding shiny things to the list every year: blouses, belts, hats, jewelry—nothing was off-limits. She gets more presents than the baby Jesus, though, so the house began sparkling from the inside out. Now, the word "shiny," in its various forms, has taken over the list.

I was looking at her list a few days before Christmas.

"Margaret, what's a *shinny belat?*"

"What number?" she answered from the other room.

By the first of December, she's memorized the entire list, so if you can't decode it, she can identify every item by its number.

"Number three," I called back.

"Oh, that's a shiny belt."

It goes on and on...*shiny show*, which were shiny shoes, *shinny swaler*, which was a shiny sweater, *shing pocky book*, shiny pocket book, and *dimond dresses*, self-explanatory.

She's not sure how to spell "shiny" so she just writes it however the mood strikes her.

One year, she put "money" and "fur coat" on the list. She didn't misspell either one.

Margaret also has a fascination, or obsession, with the Atlanta Braves baseball team. Braves memorabilia has been the subject of many Christmas lists. For the past several years, she has asked for one specific item such as a key chain, hat or nightshirt.

Last year, so as not to create confusion for anyone who might be reading the list, the very last item read, "Everything Braves."

Several years ago, Jake had a brainstorm. He wanted to drag Margaret into the 21st century. He thought she could benefit from technological advancements, so he bought her a miniature computer—you type a couple of letters on a keyboard and the machine attempts to decipher the word you want and spell it for you. No one could have imagined the chaos that would create.

If you're as hooked on phonics as Margaret is, there are no rules; you spell a word the way you sound it out. That computer was contradicting her right and left. She put it back in the box and threw it in her closet. Jake had good intentions, but anyway, why ruin the best thing about the "Christmas Lust"?

This past Christmas was no exception and the shiny presents arrived by the truckload. One of my friends left a small box at the door with no name on it. The card read: *To Margaret, From Santa Claus.* She opened it to find another gaudy piece of jewelry that she would spend hours putting on and taking off and begging Mama to let her wear to bowling.

"Now, Margaret, take that thing off, that's not for every day," Mama ordered.

"Mama, why not? It's casual."

"Casual my foot, now take it off."

After weeks of nagging, Mama finally gave in. She's mellowed quite a bit now that she's in her eighties.

"Fine. Wear the damn thing till it falls off your arm."

Margaret took Mama's directive seriously. She ate, slept and bathed in that bracelet for about six months. And then, just like that, she took it off. Margaret's stubborn. She's not going to concede until *she* has decided it's time.

"What happened to your bracelet?" I mused.

"I don't wear that bracelet every day."

"Why not?"

"Because, Embry, it's too dressy."

Living Well Lady

THE VICTORIA'S SECRET CATALOG LAY OPEN on the coffee table. Not saying a word, I smiled to myself when I noticed the dog-eared page. Then, Mama walked in and found Margaret peering intently, covetously over her glasses, her eyes glued to something. Mama's voice jolted Margaret out of her trance-like state.

"Margaret, why are you looking at that? That's Embry's magazine."

"Embry said I could look at it."

"What on earth are you looking at anyway?

"A bikini."

"Well, you can forget it. I'm not about to buy you a bikini."

"Ugh, Mama, why not?"

"Because, there'll just be too much hanging out. You need a one-piece."

"But, Mama, it's a size eighteen!"

"I don't care if it's a size forty-two, you're not gonna wear a two-piece bathing suit. Now that's the end of it."

Mama has always been on Margaret to lose weight. The odds are stacked against my sister, though—she's five feet nothing and never met a food she didn't like. Mama has served her measured portions for as long as I can remember. As a result, Margaret has had to have an affair with food and she cheats as often as possible—sneaking into the kitchen at night to scarf down ice cream or eating popcorn and drinking Coke when Mama's dozing on the couch. Just like any affair, though, she couldn't keep it up for long. Her waistline blew the whistle and something had to be done.

"Margaret, I told you about eating those snacks late at night," Mama said. "Now look what's happened. Your seat barely fits in those shorts."

Mama uses a ladylike terms for everything, so she refers to the body part that's used for sitting as a "seat." It could never be a butt, a rear end or a bottom. It's a seat.

Soon after Mama began preaching weight loss, Margaret decided she wanted to try the Jane Fonda workout album. Before we knew it, she was exercising her way into Jane Fonda oblivion. She became obsessed. She exercised day and night. She lost weight, and was in Jane Fonda shape. But that wasn't enough. She wanted to do aerobics in a real aerobics class. You can't hide anything from Margaret, if it's in vogue, she's going to know about it. Finally, Mama gave in and let her join "Living Well Lady," a local fitness and aerobics center for women only. Margaret started doing aerobics twice a week and once again, she became obsessed.

"Margaret, you have a dentist appointment on Tuesday."

"Mama, I can't. I have to go to the Living Well."

No matter what it was, it could not, *would not*, get in the way of the Living Well.

After about a month, she came home telling us they had asked her to lead the class. Neither of us could believe it, until the day Mama had something to do and I went to pick Margaret up. When I got there, she was at the front of the room, going at it. I stood around, waiting for a break in the music. Ten minutes went by, then fifteen.

I motioned with my hand and said as inconspicuously as possible, "Come on, Margaret. It's time to go."

She looked up at me through her bend-overs. "The music's not over yet."

I took a seat on the floor to wait it out. Twenty minutes later, when the class was finally over, several people came up to her.

"You did a great job, Margaret," they said. "You should lead the class every week."

The next obsession was Richard Simmons and "Sweatin' to the Oldies." Margaret had become a workout guru; she was always up on the latest fitness craze. She would work out to the Richard Simmons video in between her favorite television shows. When you watch that much television, you see every commercial that comes on.

Enter the *Easy Glider.* This was one of those exercise-at-home machines that was guaranteed to whip your body into fantastic shape. It was only a matter of time before Margaret had to have one. She started talking it up around March, so that by Christmas time, someone was sure to buy it for her. That's what she does. She talks about something incessantly so that eventually, you get it for her just so she'll stop talking about it. Jake and I were the suckers. We went to the local K-Mart and dragged the *Easy Glider* home.

Every night after supper, she would change her clothes, set the *Easy Glider* up in the living room, turn on all the lights and start pumping. It used to drive Mama crazy to think that people driving down the street could see Margaret in that skintight, hot pink leotard, exercising her way to the perfect figure.

Time goes by though and fads pass. The *Easy Glider* lasted about three months before it was folded up and pushed under a bed. Margaret started bowling on a weekly basis and then garden club, so strenuous exercise was moved to the back burner. Mama worried, so in addition to monitoring what Margaret ate, she began imposing covert weight management strategies.

"Margaret, I need you to help me rake up those leaves in the front yard."

"Mama, I can't. I've got Garden Club."

Animal Lover

MAMA HATES SQUIRRELS. SHE CALLS THEM varmints and says they're "no 'count." That's also what she says about herself when she spends the whole day doing nothing but the crossword puzzle from the newspaper in between naps on the couch.

"I haven't hit a lick all day. I'm about as no 'count as I can be."

Mama's been trying to find a way to wipe out the entire squirrel population since about 1960. Squirrels are her nemesis. She always has a garden, and it seems that the varmints can't resist a smorgasbord of fresh vegetables. When we lived in the country, Mama grew corn, squash, tomatoes, eggplant, zucchini and all kinds of peppers. She spent her life trying to get rid of the varmints that invaded her garden.

Soon, Mama didn't seem to have trouble with vegetable eaters other than squirrels—she figured out a way to deal with them. One day I came home and brought a friend with me. We pulled into the driveway to find Mama combing hair off our German shepherd and dropping it into a paper sack.

"What's she doing?" my friend asked.

Embarrassed, I mumbled, "There's no telling."

As we got closer, I gave my friend a pleading look in an attempt to communicate what I couldn't say out loud—*I'm sorry, my mama's crazy.* The air was thick, but I dove right in.

"Mama, what *are* you doing?"

"I'm putting this hair on the garden. It keeps the slugs out."

I laughed, nervously. Pointing at my friend I said, "Mama, she's gonna think you're crazy."

Without looking up at either one of us she replied, "I don't care if she does."

Then there was the time she strategically placed little plastic cups filled with urine in between her vegetable rows. That's when I decided Mama was certifiable. She claimed that rabbits don't like the smell of urine and therefore won't come near the garden. From what I understand, most people use beer, but since we didn't drink beer, Mama got creative.

"The rabbits won't know the difference," she announced. "It's all the same color."

I love animals and Mama does too, really. She just can't help herself when it comes to squirrels. As we drove through her neighborhood one Sunday afternoon, the inevitable happened.

Even though I did everything I could to avoid it, I hit one of the varmints as it darted across the road. I looked in the rearview mirror and saw the poor little creature still moving.

"Oh, I need to do something, Mama. It's still alive."

"Don't you turn around now," she said. "Just keep driving."

Now that she lives in town again, Mama tries to grow a small crop of tomatoes when summer rolls around. Every year, I hear the same complaint. "Those damn squirrels just ruin everything."

She's right, though—the varmint will take a small bite out of a perfectly good tomato and then drop it on the ground. After several years of ruined tomatoes, frustration set in.

At first, she tried shooting them with one of Jake's old pellet guns. That did nothing but make the squirrel mad and want to come back for more. The pellets, when she actually hit a squirrel with one, bounced off the varmint and hit the ground.

Finally, she set up a trap that looked like it could catch a small dog. Every day she would go out and check it, and one day there it was, the first trapped squirrel. The problem was, the varmint wasn't dead, just trapped. So Mama, being the resourceful woman that she is, filled up a big plastic trash can with water and dropped the trap into the trash can, squirrel and all.

One day, my curiosity got the best of me.

"What did you do with those squirrels after you drowned them?"

Mama smiled a crafty smile. "I dropped 'em down the sewer."

Thank goodness the city hadn't posted a sign proclaiming there will be no getting rid of varmints in the sewer system. Mama really does love animals, as long as they're not those of the pesky, tomato ruining, varmint variety.

Plain Wooden Box

MAMA ALWAYS LOOKS IN THE PAPER to see who died. I know most old people do that, and I understand it—I just can't help but wonder if they all subject some member of their family to what I call the funeral diatribe: "Now, Embry, don't y'all spend a lot of money on a casket for me. I don't want those people at my funeral saying, 'Oh look at Augusta, she just had to have that fancy casket.'"

Mama is real concerned about not putting on airs. I suppose she might also think it would be "common" to have a fancy casket. Mama is adamantly opposed to being common.

One weekend, I was home visiting and she started in on the casket speech. After a leisurely breakfast, I sipped coffee while Mama perused the newspaper.

"Now y'all just get me a plain casket."

"What are you talking about?" I asked.

"I'm talking about my funeral. All I need is a plain wooden box."

"Why does it matter what kind of casket you're buried in?"

"Well, I just don't need something fancy. I'm not gonna be in it anyway."

"Where do you think you're gonna be?"

"Well, my bones are gonna be in it, but I don't plan on staying."

Margaret gets worried when Mama starts talking about dying. I don't know if Margaret truly understands death; even though some of her adult friends have died at exceptionally young ages, she usually talks about their passing as if they've gone on vacation.

"Oh did you hear about Susan?" Mama says.

"No," I reply.

"She died," Margaret adds. She may as well have said, "She went to Panama City."

She must know something, though, because whenever Mama starts talking about funerals and dying, Margaret gets disturbed.

"Mama, I don't want you to die. What about me?"

"Well, what about you?" Mama replies.

"Who's gonna take me to bowling?"

Mama's obsession with death continues with a love of cemeteries. This seems to be a uniquely Southern phenomenon. Southerners love to go walk around in a cemetery, and just about any cemetery will do.

In our hometown of Columbus, Georgia, a group of people have started a foundation to raise money for the preservation of the oldest cemetery in town. They actually send out a newsletter to inform you of the goings on at the cemetery. Of course, almost all of our kinfolk are buried there, so Mama had to join up. In the fall, they send out an invitation to "ramble" through the cemetery and enjoy libations to boot. How funny it must be to see those old drunk folks wandering through the cemetery, commenting on the personal lives of the dearly departed.

After I finished graduate school, Mama, Margaret and I took a trip to Savannah. On our way across the entire state of Georgia, we passed through several small towns. At about the midway point, I noticed a large cemetery on the side of the road. Mama looked out the window and exclaimed, "Oh, they sure do have a lot of dead people here."

Our first day of sightseeing in Savannah began, only by chance, with a tour through one of the town's oldest cemeteries. We were driving along taking in the sights.

"Now stop up here, Embry, I want to see this cemetery."

Why on earth would she want to wander around in a cemetery in Savannah, I wondered. *She doesn't know a single soul here, alive or dead.* As it turns out, one of her favorite authors writes about Savannah and many of its prominent families. Supposedly, they were buried in this cemetery. Needless to say, the homes they actually lived in were not nearly as interesting as their addresses now that they were dead.

Southerners know, most any cemetery will do.

Dressed to Rest

MARGARET AND MAMA HAVE A PECULIAR, unhealthy relationship with clothing. They both wear the same clothes for several days in a row; however, Mama makes Margaret change her clothes more often because she actually leaves the house. Mama, on the other hand, spends a lot of time sitting. When she does move, it's slow. Her clothes don't get much exposure to the elements. This economical way of living gives her license to exercise parental rights.

"Now, Margaret, you need to put that dress in the dirty clothes. You've been wearing it so much it could stand alone."

"Mama, a dress can't stand alone."

Margaret's smart. She caught on quickly and found a way around the system. She now picks out two sets of clothes each day, those for staying in and those for going out.

A few years ago, Mama bought Margaret two bright colored, cotton sundresses. She loved them and, of course, wanted to wear one every day. She immediately decided that these two articles of clothing would be her staying-in attire. She even gave them a name.

"That's a cute dress, Marg."

"It's not a dress, Embry. It's a muumuu."

When it's warm outside, she wears one or the other every day.

95

This clothing ritual, along with her daily routine are about the most predictable events in the universe—enough to make Father Time relinquish his title.

I don't know how it works, but Margaret wakes up every morning at 9:00; not one minute before, not one minute after, 9:00, sharp.

She gets up, pours herself some juice, fixes cereal or yogurt, and on occasion, a Slim Fast. Don't talk to her, though—she's incapable of responding until she's had her decaf coffee.

After she finishes eating, she re-heats her coffee in the microwave at least six times, and even though this has been going on every day for fifteen years, Mama preaches on.

"Margaret, I told you to finish that coffee. Stop totin' it around now and drink it!"

"Mama, I am drinking it!"

Then, she washes her face, brushes her teeth and puts on the muumuu. When it's time to go somewhere, she takes off the muumuu and puts on shorts and a T-shirt. This drives Mama bonkers.

"Margaret, I don't know why you've got to change clothes all day long. Why did you take that dress off?"

"Ugh, Mama, you told me to take it off!"

During the winter, Mama gets in bed at night and lays her clothes out on top of her, just as if she was wearing them. Usually a turtleneck or a sweatshirt, which she lays over her chest, and whatever pants she wore that day stretched out over her legs.

I walked into her room one night and there she lay, eyes closed, arms crossed over her chest, her former self, albeit somewhat flat, laid out on top of her. I stood there thinking, my gosh, she's laid herself to rest!

I didn't want to startle her, but the eeriness of it forced me to speak. "Mama, why do you have your clothes on top of you like that?

Coming out of her funeral-like pose, she opened her eyes and calmly said, "They're keepin' me warm."

"Why don't you just get a blanket?" I asked.

"That's too much trouble," she drawled. "Besides, this way I can put 'em back on before I get out the bed in the mawnin'."

She's taken the concept of energy conservation to new heights, I thought.

Then, summer comes and I realize there is no ceiling.

"Mama, you need to turn the air down. It's hot in here."

"Well, sit still," she says.

"Great," I say under my breath. "I'm just going to melt into a puddle of sweat."

She gives me a sideways glance and says, "If you're that hot, take off some clothes."

Black Cord Fever

"MARGARET, ANSWER THE PHONE." MAMA LIKES to give orders.

From her bedroom comes Margaret's standard response to the phone ringing. "I hope that's not for me."

From the den comes Mama's response to Margaret. "You know good and well it's for you, now pick up the phone!"

After several protests, Margaret gives in. "Hello?...Oh, hey, Beth."

If the phone's ringing, more often than not it's for Margaret. Her friends are numerous and quite colorful, and for some odd reason, they've all been stricken with what one of my teachers used to call black cord fever.

Margaret met Beth Walton in Dee Rainey's class. They've been friends going on thirty-five years and for almost that long, Margaret has done everything Beth says. That's not such a bad thing for Margaret, she's rather passive and needs a strong influence in her life. Besides, they have lots of things in common and Beth is a loyal friend; she's just, well...bossy.

When they were teenagers, Beth would call several times a day almost every day. Sometimes she called and as soon as someone said hello, she'd hang up. Other times, she called and actually had things to say; still others, she'd call and send Margaret on a wild-goose chase.

This was before the cordless, so changing phones required a team effort. Mama or I would answer the phone. "Margaret, it's for you."

The game was on.

Beth would always give Margaret time to get comfortable before she began giving orders, then, within minutes, came the request for backup.

"Embry, can you hang up this phone?"

"Why?"

"Beth told me to go to the kitchen," she'd say in an exasperated tone.

Margaret didn't dare disobey an order. I'd go to the bedroom and hold the phone until she got to the kitchen.

"Okay, Embry, you can hang it up now."

Margaret traipsed from kitchen to bedroom to den, at least until Daddy got home—game over. If Daddy noticed the phone off the cradle, he'd hang it up whether the conversation was finished or not. He didn't have much patience for things of this nature, whereas Mama and I found it entertaining. We'd make bets on how many trips Margaret would make around the house.

Over the years, Beth's phone calls have slacked off, although every now and then, she still calls and hangs up without saying anything. Most people would worry about someone calling and hanging up, not at Mama's house—it's probably Beth.

Beth's mellowed with age, though, and these days, she doesn't hang up as quickly.

I found this out when I answered the phone at Mama's house. "Hello?…Hello?" I said, holding the line for a minute or so. No hang up, just silence. I went out on a limb. "Beth?"

A voice answered from the other end, "What?!"

"Did you want to speak to Margaret?" I asked.

"Yes."

"She's not here."

Click, no more Beth. When Beth calls, she wants to talk to Margaret—not me, not Mama, not anyone other than her good friend Margaret.

Most of Margaret's friends call to chat, but at some point, almost everyone in her group will call to verify a tidbit of vital information, to get the last word.

"Yes, that's right, swimming is at 9:00. It's on the calendar," Margaret says with all the authority of a born leader.

Margaret, along with everyone else in her recreation group, receives a calendar each month outlining activities on a weekly basis. Included is a newsletter about upcoming events and trips, as well as everyone's name who has a birthday that month. The calendar may as well be known as the King James version—at least to Margaret. If it's on the calendar, it's the gospel. But as much as the calendar is the Word to Margaret, she is Moses to her people.

John Allen Corbin, a longtime friend of hers who also has Down syndrome, calls every night at ten after eight. You can set your clock by him. Mama says he calls because he likes for Margaret to read the calendar to him. I think he calls because he's sweet on her. John Allen has a wonderful personality and is always ready to chat. If I happen to answer the phone, he'll go into his charming mode. "Oh, Embry, I've been missing you. I'm glad you're back."

After our conversation, I asked Margaret if what Mama said was true. "Margaret, does John Allen get you to read the calendar to him?"

"No," she replied. "He just likes to talk about bowling and everything else."

"He knows how to read, doesn't he?"

She gave me a serious look and said, "He wears glasses, he ought to."

The phone rings and Margaret whines again, "I hope that's not for me." It seems that she's relegated to a life of black cord fever, though, the phone's always for her, only this time, it's someone she wants to talk to. Unfortunately, Mama's back to giving orders.

"Margaret, hang up the phone."

"Mama, I'm still talking."

"I don't care, hang it up."

100

Talking Television

MAMA GREW UP IN A TIME when people in the South spoke true southern English, a slow, lilting, beautiful dialect untainted by outside influences. She doesn't acknowledge the letter "r" unless it has the audacity to find itself at the beginning of a word, so when she says Margaret's name, it comes out sounding more like "Maahgret."

Mama's disappointed that none of her children have carried on the family dialect; so disappointed in fact, she brings it to our attention whenever possible. When she hears any of us, which usually means me, giving a word its due, she rolls her eyes and starts the lecture.

"I don't know why y'all have to talk television."

"What's that supposed to mean?" I say.

"You talk like those people do on television, not southern, like you ought to."

It's no wonder we talk television. For the first twenty-five years of her life, Margaret was obsessed. She watched it as much as Mama would allow, talked about it the rest of the time, and memorized the TV listings. She became a walking, talking *TV Guide*. All you had to do was name a program.

"Margaret, *Hawaii Five-O*."

"Tuesday night, eight o'clock, channel nine."

When we were in elementary school, playing outdoors was the only option after school. Mama wasn't going to hear of us coming home and plopping down in front of the television. Once we moved to Alabama, though, things changed. Life slows down when you move to the country—you have to create entertainment. Margaret turned on the television and turned off everything and everybody else. She watched every afternoon after school, took a break for supper, then watched from 6:30 until 10:00, without fail. Finally, Mama tried to curb the addiction.

"Margaret, you need to go outside and walk up and down the driveway a few times. You've been sitting in front of that television for too long."

"Mama, I can't... *To Tell the Truth* comes on in five minutes."

"Well, that's five minutes of walking."

Margaret's uncanny knowledge of the TV schedule allowed for complete domination over our nightly viewing, not to mention, she had strict orders from Beth.

"Margaret, I wanna watch *Charlie's Angels.*"

"Embry, that's on channel nine."

"So?"

"Beth says I have to watch channel three."

Beth's Daddy worked at the CBS station in Columbus so Margaret was limited in her program selection.

"If Beth Walton jumped into the Chattahoochee, would you jump too?"

I'd wanted to say that for seventeen years. Finally, I had a chance to use one of Mama's famous one-liners.

Margaret looked at me and shook her head. "Embry, Beth doesn't like to swim."

Foolishness

FOR YEARS, I'D WONDERED WHERE MARGARET learned to drink coffee. Somehow, without anybody knowing it, she got hooked on the stuff and now has to have her fix every morning. I couldn't figure it out, though, because we never had coffee growing up. I don't even remember Mama or Daddy drinking coffee, although I'm sure they did. Even so, we weren't allowed to have any and I knew that Margaret must have seen someone else drinking it and copied them.

That's how Margaret picks things up. She watches and then she copies. That's why Mama tries to monitor, as much as possible, everything Margaret sees, hears or does. She knows Margaret has the memory of an elephant.

One weekend when I was visiting, I rented *Forrest Gump* for Mama and Margaret. Mama won't watch a movie on her own, she says it's a waste of time. She's seen one movie on the big screen in forty years—*Steel Magnolias*, and that was only because one of her friends dragged her to the theatre. So, I got the movie, sat Mama down and gave instructions. "Watch this," I said, "I think you'll enjoy it."

Reluctantly, Mama sat down on the couch and Margaret pulled her chair up in front of the television, two feet from the screen. For a while, everything was fine and Mama acted like she was enjoying the story, even though she was fumbling around with the newspaper. That lasted only until the scene in which Forrest visits his girlfriend Jenny at college, and she decides to show him what it's like to be with a girl. About the time Jenny took off her shirt and put Forrest's hand on her bra-clad breast, Mama looked up from the funny pages.

"Now, Margaret, this is just a movie," she stated in her most motherly tone. "People don't really do that."

"Mama, I know it's a movie," Margaret whined.

Mama shot me a look and muttered, "You didn't tell me we were going to be watching foolishness such as that."

"Don't worry," I said. "There aren't any more scenes like that one."

Deciding she was no longer interested, Mama focused her attention on the daily crossword puzzle. Margaret stayed glued to the TV screen and I watched in silence, even though I knew Mama was covertly monitoring the rest of the movie. She knows Margaret watches and then she copies.

Evidently, Margaret's not the only one. Linda Jones, who recently retired from the recreation department after many years of running the T.R. program, told me how Margaret and John Allen decided to copy a scene from the movie *Dirty Dancing*.

During a weekend trip to Special Olympics, all of the athletes were treated to a movie night. They were supposed to watch something light and of no consequence, but there was a snafu and *Dirty Dancing* was the backup movie. At the dance the following night, Margaret and John Allen put on their own dirty dancing show for everyone in attendance.

According to Linda, through some strange coincidence, the D.J. played the song "Hungry Eyes," the title song from *Dirty Dancing*. John Allen and Margaret were on opposite sides of the room, but when the music started, they began moving toward each other in a scene reminiscent of the movie. They finally met in the middle of the gym floor and after much posturing and trying to figure out what to do next, they gave up and danced the only way they knew how—holding hands and rocking back and forth from right foot to left foot. Linda said she'd never forget it as long as she lived.

The same day that Linda told me that story, I ran into Beth Walton's sister Brenda. We were all attending a Special Olympics bowling tournament in Columbus. I told Brenda about the book I was writing and we began sharing stories about Margaret and Beth.

"Did you know that Margaret used to drink a whole pot of coffee every Saturday morning when she stayed at our house?" Brenda said.

Finally, the coffee mystery was solved. Margaret had spent almost every Friday night for fifteen years with Beth. So for fifteen years, she sat at the Walton's kitchen table on Saturday morning and copied them drinking coffee. Brenda said they thought Margaret drank coffee at home. She seemed like such a pro, they figured she knew what she was doing.

What Mr. and Mrs. Walton didn't take into account was that if they had smoked cigarettes, drank moonshine and cursed like sailors, Margaret would have done that too, because she watches and then she copies.

Love Boat

MARGARET ALWAYS SAID SHE WAS GOING to marry Jonathan Davis. A sweet, soft-spoken young man with Down syndrome, he was delightful to be around.

Margaret and Jonathan met in first grade, in Dee Rainey's class. They became fast friends and before long, what most people would refer to as an item. Well, as much of an item as our Mama and his Mama would allow.

Margaret and Jonathan did everything together. They'd go to movies, go skating or just spend time watching television. As they got older, they traveled together to Special Olympics and shared bowling, arts and crafts, and pottery classes through the recreation department.

What I remember most about Jonathan were his beautiful manners. He opened doors for Margaret, he always let her walk a step ahead, he said "yes, ma'am" and "no, ma'am" to Mama. He was the ultimate boyfriend.

When Margaret was in her early twenties, prime marrying years, *The Love Boat* was the most popular show on television. She never missed an episode and sailing on the famed ship became her life's mission.

"Jonathan and I are going on the Love Boat," she said to me one night at supper.

"That's great, Marg. How are you going to do that?"

"Mama's going to take us."

Mama's ear was peeled. "I'm not about to do any such thing."

"Ugh, Mama, why not?"

"Now, Margaret, you don't need to go on the Love Boat," Mama said. "Besides, you and Jonathan are just friends." Mama was reaching. "Friends don't go on the Love Boat."

"Mama, Jonathan and I are going to get married," Margaret replied. "Anyway, that's what you're supposed to do in your twenties."

For the first time in her life, Mama was thanking her lucky stars that neither I, also in my twenties, nor my brother, well into his thirties, had gotten married. Mama used her best ammunition. "Jake's not married, and neither is Embry."

"I know that," Margaret exclaimed.

"Well, you're not gettin' married either. Now I don't wanna hear any more about it."

Margaret didn't argue. She just kept watching her show every week. I know she dreamed of sailing on that magical cruise ship with her one true love. I could see it in her eyes as she sat glued to the television screen.

Soon, Jonathan got a job at Burger King and he was too busy to participate in any of the group activities or spend time with Margaret. Just like that, no more Jonathan.

Margaret didn't seem to be too upset about it—she found other things to keep herself busy—volunteer work, bowling, Garden Club, answering the phone twenty-five times a day.

Many years after *The Love Boat* went off the air, Mama decided to surprise Margaret and take her on a cruise. Mama, Margaret and Mama's sister Isabel and her husband Joe drove to Tampa and boarded a cruise ship to Mexico.

On the way out, the ship went through a wicked storm and Mama said everyone on the boat was sick. Everyone except Margaret. She was the only one in line at the buffet table. Life was good. All the food she could eat, and on the Love Boat to boot.

After the trip to Mexico, Mama and I were sure Margaret had her fill of cruises.

We certainly thought the Love Boat was a distant memory, and marriage, that was definitely in the past. She hadn't talked about getting married for years. She even told somebody the reason she wasn't married was because she had a Magnolia tree in her front yard and she didn't have time for a husband because she spent all of her time picking up Magnolia leaves. Then, the lottery came to Georgia and *TV Land* came to cable.

"If I win the lottery, I'm going to take my whole family on a cruise."

"Why a cruise, Margaret? Let's go to Hawaii!" I said.

"Embry, the Love Boat doesn't go to Hawaii."

"What made you think of the Love Boat?" I said.

"I watch it all the time."

"The Love Boat?!" I exclaimed.

"Yes. Tuesday night, 9:00, channel fifty-four."

The Reckoning

MY FAMILY LIKES TO THINK OF themselves as late bloomers. We don't like to say that we just take our time or that we can't seem to get it together—no, we say we're late bloomers. The truth is, we do things slower than most people.

Mama didn't start teaching school until she was well into her forties, I went back to graduate school in my late thirties and Jake didn't get married until he was forty. Late bloomers? I don't think so, we're just slow.

Jake and Julie had been dating on and off for seven years. We all hoped a wedding was in their future, but nobody was willing to place a wager on it. Mostly, we just whispered about it behind closed doors. Too much talking might have hurt Jake's chances.

I was home from Miami for several days during the Christmas holidays. Jake and Julie came over for what we thought was an ordinary visit, but as soon as they walked into the den, I knew something was up. Jake had a grin as wide as the Chattahoochee on his face and Julie stood next to him smiling, tentatively.

My sister-in-law doesn't do anything tentatively, although I noticed that on that particular day, she did look nervous. I was able to make this judgment about Julie because I had known her much longer than my brother had. She and I are the same age and had gone to school together since the fifth grade.

After looking awkward for several minutes, Jake announced that they were engaged and would be getting married some time the following year. We all gushed over them and I cried. My big brother was finally getting married, and to a woman he had been smitten with since day one. I thought back to the first time he went out with her. He was thirty-four. Julie and I were only twenty-three.

"Guess who I had a date with?" he casually said to me one day when he stopped by the house to do something for Mama.

"I have no idea," I replied, wondering why in the world he would think I'd know anyone he was going out with.

"Julie Adams," he said with a big, kind of dumb-looking grin on his face.

"Julie Adams?! Jake, she's *my* age."

"I know that," he snapped. "Anyway, it was just a date. I didn't say I was going to marry her!"

My reaction was based on my brother's behavior toward me ever since I had been old enough to have a conversation with him. He had always looked out for me, watched over me and, at times, even bossed me around. He treated me more like I was his child than his sister. Then, when I was old enough to hang out with him, he always introduced me to his friends the same way.

"I'd like you to meet Embry," he'd say. "She's my baby sister."

He had always made it clear that he was the much older brother. My reaction to his dating someone my age was justified.

The wedding would take place on a beautiful day in May and was greatly anticipated by all 250 people in attendance. Jake's friends as well as Mama and Daddy's were elated that Jake, a kind, handsome and, up until now, very eligible bachelor was finally settling down. They turned out in droves to witness the event.

Even though most everyone was overcome with the knowledge that Jake was actually getting married and just happy to be part of the festivities, there were those who added a different spin to the situation. At the rehearsal dinner, our cousin Tom, who has always been close to Jake, stood up to make the first toast.

"There's something to be said for waiting until you're forty years old to get married," he quipped. Holding his glass in the air, he said, "You're not married *most* of your life." Tom's humor broke the ice and the rest of the evening was filled with toasts to the oldest bachelor in the room.

The sun was high in the sky when the wedding started and by 2:00, everyone was on their way to the Columbus Country Club for the reception. Food and drink were abundant and Margaret, like everyone else, was giddy with the excitement of it all. Somehow, she got loose from me and Mama and no one was monitoring her movements. Three champagne glasses later, Margaret was dancing with everyone and anyone every time the band played.

"Margaret sure is having a good time," someone said to me as we watched her cuttin' a rug on the dance floor.

"Yeah, that Margaret really knows how to party," I said. "She has a good time wherever she goes."

As I made my way to the rest room, I noticed that Mama had perched herself in a chair for the duration. Sipping a glass of champagne, she purveyed the room and chatted with my aunt and uncle. The band continued to play to a packed dance floor for the next couple of hours and then, much too soon, the newlyweds were leaving.

We gathered outside to say our last goodbyes as Jake and Julie sped off to the airport. Margaret threw birdseed and Mama smiled and waved. We stood outside for a while visiting with friends and relatives we hadn't seen in years. Finally, I went to get the car and came back to find them waiting on the steps.

"Okay, party's over," I said. "Come on, you two, time to go."

Within minutes, Margaret was passed out in the back seat and Mama was looking peeked.

"Are you okay?" I said, thinking she must have been overwhelmed by the day's events.

"I'm feeling a little lightheaded," she drawled.

"Well now, looks like Margaret wasn't the only one who found the champagne," I chuckled.

Mama's delivery was slower than usual. "Maahgaret's been drinking champagne?"

"Oh yeah, and lots of it," I said, nodding my head in the direction of the back seat.

"Well, that's alright," Mama said. "I don't reckon we have days like this very often."

"No," I said. "I don't reckon we do."

The Jar

MAMA COULD HOLD A LIFETIME MEMBERSHIP in the Society of Self-Effacing Southern Women, if there was such a thing. The society's members would have dwindled significantly by now, though, not just because they're old, but because there's not anyone to take their places. No, there aren't any young modern women who can self efface like Mama's generation—today's women are too busy self-medicating to be self-deprecating.

You see, women like my mama are the masters of self-deprecation. No matter what anyone tells them, they downplay their looks, their smarts and, of course, any God-given talents they might possess. They don't talk about themselves, or their children for that matter, because that would be bragging, and bragging is a major faux pas in the society of self-effacing women, or should I say ladies.

"My Lawud, I look like who shot John," Mama drawls. She's just glanced at herself in the mirror.

"Mama, you look great. I don't know why you talk about yourself like that."

She turns a keen eye on me. "I've been looking at myself a lot longer than you have."

Her personal affront notwithstanding, my mother is a striking woman. She has beautiful features, is tall and athletic, and looks great in her clothes—attributes most women would die for.

When she was young, she looked like she could have stepped right out of *J. Crew* or *Land's End*, without wearing a stitch of makeup. To this day, her idea of fixing herself up is putting on a little lipstick and running a comb through her hair.

"Are you ready to go, Mama?" I call from the den.

"Almost," she says. "Let me put on some lipstick."

I can hear her fumbling around with something. "We need to get going, Mama, we're gonna' be late for church."

I walk into her bathroom and find her staring into the mirror. "Oooh, I bettuh put on some rouge," she says. "I need a little culuh."

I'm surprised she's taking the time to put on rouge. She usually doesn't look at herself in the mirror long enough to notice these things. She means to look decent and presentable, but she's not going to spend a lot of time doing it. With Mama, what you see is what you get.

Her friends and family are lucky, though, because what you get with Mama is a very attractive woman who's also smart, witty and down to earth. She tells it like it is, or at least how she sees it. And most of the time, it's downright entertaining.

I came home from Miami after a six-month absence. My hair was longer than usual, curly, and basically out of control. After I'd been in the house for about five minutes, Mama circled me and said, "Good Lawud, Embry, a rat would swim the Chattahoochee to get in yo hayuh."

I retorted and she tried to pass the buck. "That was one of your daddy's favorite things to say."

She claims that most of her good sayings came from Daddy, but Mama has some doozies of her own. And hers have that certain something, let's see, how do I say it...oh yeah, that self-deprecating quality that could only come from a product of Mama's generation.

"When I was in college, my friends and I had lots of funny sayings," Mama announced out of the blue.

"About what?" I asked.

"Oh, all kinds of things, but one in particular was my favorite."

"Oh yeah, well, let's hear it," I said.

A devious smile played across her face as she began reciting:

> *"I know how ugly I are.*
> *I know my face ain't no star.*
> *But I don't mind it, 'cause I'm behind it*
> *It's the ones in the front get the jar."*

Milestones

"WE HAVE TO DO SOMETHING SPECIAL for Margaret's fortieth birthday," I said to Mama one day in December a few years ago. "This is really something, can you believe she's going to be forty years old?"

Mama doesn't get real excited about birthdays, never has, in fact. But even she acknowledged this one deserved celebrating.

"Whatever you want to do is fine with me," she said. "You've always been so good to her and I sure do appreciate it."

The event wasn't necessarily special because someone was turning forty; it was special because that someone was Margaret. Hadn't I heard that people with Down syndrome only have a life expectancy of around thirty-five years? Isn't that what we *always* heard? Even though my big sister had defied the odds her entire life—no heart or respiratory problems, walking and talking at almost the same time as typically developing children, learning to read and write, participating in Special Olympics well into her thirties—still in the back of my mind was the lingering doubt about her well-being. The wondering, the wanting to know... how long will she be around?

I don't remember much about Margaret's twentieth, twenty-fifth, or even her thirtieth birthdays. I was too lost in the egocentricity that was my life. I was just starting college, graduating from college or taking off on an adventure that would cause Mama to have a hissy fit when I told her about it.

"What do you mean you're moving to Miami?"

I thought I was going to have to peel her off the ceiling.

Then, on their first visit to South Florida, Mama brought Margaret into the fray by telling her about the Cuban people who live in Miami, how they speak a foreign language and eat strange food. Margaret looked worried.

"Is Embry going to turn into a Cuban?" she asked Mama as they drove across the southern tip of Florida into Dade County.

I had been caught up in my life for a long time, but now I was home and becoming more involved in what was going on with my family. My mother was getting older and time with her was precious. I missed her and Margaret and I realized how significant this birthday was. This was forty!

I decided the party had to be grand, at least by Margaret's definition. After much contemplation, I came to the conclusion that as far as she was concerned, that meant two things—food in unlimited quantities, and beer—anything beyond that was gravy.

On the Saturday before her birthday, I drove Margaret to Atlanta where a group of my friends who know and love her dearly met us at a Mexican restaurant. There, she was free to eat and drink to her heart's content, something Mama would never let her do.

What I didn't realize was that Margaret could have spent the entire night in the same spot as long as someone kept bringing her enchiladas and Miller Lite. After a couple of hours, I knew I had to do something to get her up from that table. I'd never hear the end of it if I brought her home sick the next day with a hangover, even though I only let her have two beers, which she nursed like they were the last two on earth.

"Hey, Margaret," I said, noticing she had only a few morsels of food left on her plate. "What do you say we go line dancing?"

Still chewing, she smiled and said, "Okay, let's party!"

Margaret loves music and she's wild about dancing. She was taking line dancing every Monday morning at the church, so she was excited about trying out her new country dancing feet.

Several years ago, someone gave Margaret a *Non-Stop Macarena* CD for Christmas; an entire CD of nothing but that one song, played over and over and over. She danced day and night and night and day. She danced the Macarena until Mama was forced to intervene.

"Margaret, you're about to drive me slap crazy!" Mama walked into the living room, took the CD out, turned off the player and declared, "That's enough."

That was the end of the Macarena. Line dancing was a welcomed diversion.

Margaret's birthday bash was a huge hit. A chance to gorge herself on Mexican food, drink not one but two beers, and to top it off, dancing. After an hour or so of Cotton-Eyed Joe, Boot-Scootin' Boogie and the Texas Two-Step, she asked for another beer. I went to the bar and ordered an *O'Doul's*. She took one look at it and said, "That's nonalcoholic."

Margaret sang, danced and giggled her way into the next day, completely lost in the celebration of her fortieth year of life. In the wee hours of the morning, we drove to a friend's house to spend the night. After we climbed into the small double bed, I snuggled close to Margaret and silently replayed the events of the day. I lay awake that night for a long time wondering if all the pomp and circumstance had been more for me than for her. Finally, I closed my eyes and thanked God for my sister.

On our way back home the next day, I was reminded of how oblivious Margaret is to the miraculous nature of her existence. I looked over and found her dozing, as usual.

"Well, how does it feel to be forty?" I asked.

Through half-closed eyes came her reply. "Next year I'll be forty-one. What can we do for my birthday next year?"

I smiled and pictured God smiling too. The celebration had indeed been a much bigger deal to me than it was to her. But then, how could it not be? Margaret celebrates life every day.

World's Greatest Aunt

WHEN JAKE AND JULIE ANNOUNCED THEY were having a baby, Mama, overwhelmed by the thought of actually becoming a grandparent at the age of seventy-nine, turned over a new leaf.

She stopped complaining about taking her medicine. She bought baby clothes, baby toys, and baby books. She insisted that Jake and I nearly kill ourselves dragging a fifty-year-old crib down from her attic. She even talked about taking pictures.

Mama doesn't take pictures. She doesn't even like to look at pictures somebody else has taken. She'll pretend she's interested, casually sorting through them, pausing every now and then to say, "hmm," when she's really thinking, "I don't have time for this. I could be doing the crossword puzzle."

Margaret's the camera buff in the family. She always has two or three cameras lying around—a couple of disposables and a real one that's on the blink. And pictures galore, interesting ones at that—the bed she slept in on one of her outings across the state, some strange looking plant at a Garden Club of Georgia convention, my dining room table. Sometimes, even a random person or two.

Margaret loves to take pictures, Mama does not. The only time I've ever seen Mama with a camera is when someone has stuck one in her hand and asked her to do the honors. Her disdain

119

inevitably shows up in the finished product—someone's head is always cut off.

Needless to say, when Felix Jacob Burrus, III (Jake) was born, the world became a different place, especially for Margaret and Mama. They started keeping the baby two or three days a week, and, before long, you couldn't get him away from either one of them.

"Ma-ma," which is what he calls Margaret, became the greatest person in the history of the world. "Googa," which is what he calls Mama, ran a very close second. "Emmy," which is what he started calling me after several people forced him to acknowledge my existence, wasn't even a blip on the radar.

For the first year of little Jake's life, whenever he was in Mama and Margaret's company, he wanted nothing to do with anyone else, especially me.

I told myself, "He's not used to you yet, he doesn't see you as often. He'd love you if he just got to know you."

Margaret, in her sweet, adoring way, would try to help me out. "Do you want to hold him, Embry?"

"Yes, I'd love to, but he doesn't like me."

"Yes, he does. You like her, don't you, Jakey?"

I'd reach my arms out in hopeful anticipation and he'd tune up like a big band. Grabbing onto Margaret, he'd just stare at me and scream.

No matter what I did to try and win the world's greatest aunt award, it was futile. Margaret had it sewn up. What better playmate could a two-year-old have than a bona fide grown-up with the heart and soul of someone his own age? What could possibly top having an adult who will play whatever you want, as long as you want, and never say, "Okay, let's do something else, daddy's old and he's tired."

It was obvious, Jake's heart belonged to Margaret, and since home is where the heart is, Googa's house is still the coolest place in the world.

Now that he's older, he's warmed up to me, and, recently, Mama said he even asked about me, out of the blue. I couldn't believe it. I thought, *It's a miracle! He loves me. He knows I'm a real person.*

Now *I* was overwhelmed. I knew how Mama felt. I wanted to go out and buy little boy clothes and little boy toys, but I told myself, *Don't go overboard, this adoration may not last.* Instead, I thought, *I'll give him a call. He loves to talk on the phone, and after all, he asked about me.*

I dialed my brother's number so I could talk to my nephew.

"Jake," my brother said. "It's Emmy, do you want to talk to her?"

"Yes, I do," came his reply.

I was smiling all over when his sweet little voice came on the phone.

"Hello?" he said.

"Hey, Jake, it's Emmy."

"Hey, Emmy."

"How are you?" I asked.

"Fine," he said in his little boy voice. "Emmy, are you at Googa's house?"

Time and Temperature

MARGARET'S NEVER BEEN ONE FOR PICKING out greeting cards. She likes to make her own. Sometimes she uses blank cards and writes a sweet, formal note. Other times, a folded piece of construction paper adorned with an original artistic creation does the trick. Mama makes her write a thank-you note for everything, so she's well equipped with a supply of cards, paper and writing utensils.

One card in particular comes to mind right away, a Valentine card that read: *Dear Embry, you are a sweethart. You are. Love, Margaret Burrus.*

Margaret always signs her first and last name, even if the card's for someone in our family, and since becoming obsessed with the weather, she puts the temperature in the top right corner.

The first time I received a "weather card" was when I finished graduate school. I smiled as I opened the blue construction paper.

Congratulations, Embry. I'm proud of you for your graduation.
I love you, you my sweet sister.

I knew that Mama had spelled "congratulations" and "graduation" for her. If Margaret needs help with spelling, Mama writes the word and then has Margaret copy it onto the card. The sweet and thoughtful part, she had done on her own.

After staring at the card for several minutes, I noticed a mystery word in the top corner. *What could "godurgrels" mean?* I said to myself. Next to the mystery word was a bright yellow sun drawn with crayon. I looked back and forth from the picture to the word, baffled.

Anxious to solve the mystery, I took the card with me the next time I went home to visit.

"Hey, Margaret, what does this say on my card?" I asked.

"What?" she replied.

"This," I said, pointing to the mystery word.

"Oh," she said, peering over her glasses, "Ninety degrees."

The way she had written it, the "9" in "90" looked like a lower case "g" and the number "90" and the word "degrees," misspelled of course, were all jumbled together, hence, *godurgrels*.

"Why did you put that on my card?" I asked.

"It was hot outside."

After showing that card to several people and relating the story behind it, I found that people love these stories about Margaret and remember her made-up words. One of my friends walked outside on a scorching summer day and exclaimed, "Wow, it's godurgrels out here!"

Margaret's obsession with temperature is born of the fact that she and Mama watch *The Weather Channel* all hours of the day and night. Actually, the first thing Margaret does when she gets up in the morning is turn on *The Weather Channel.* And unless it's time for *A Wedding Story*, *A Dating Story*, or *A Baby Story*, Margaret's three favorite daytime shows, *The Weather Channel* is usually blaring.

"We've got sixty-two today," she'll announce in the morning after she's finished her breakfast. "Party cloudy with a forty percent chance of rain..." She reads every piece of information as it scrolls across the screen. And I thought only old people were obsessed with time and temperature; old people and Margaret.

Margaret's therapeutic recreation program, which she calls "T.R.," provides door-to-door van service for anybody who doesn't have transportation to most of the weekly activities; however, Margaret doesn't usually ride on the van—she has Mama. But, if Mama has a doctor's appointment or is going to lunch with one of her younger sisters who live in town, Margaret takes the van.

During my vacation last year, I decided to visit them in the middle of the week. I drove up to find Margaret, along with her bowling bag, sitting in the driveway.

"Hey, Tooks," I greeted, giving her a hug. "What are you doing out here in the driveway?"

"I'm waiting on Linda to pick me up."

"Why is she picking you up?"

"I'm on the pickup list."

Okay, I thought. *I'll play.* "I know, but why are you on the list? Why isn't Mama taking you to bowling?"

"Mama has to go to the doctor."

"What time is the van picking you up?" I asked.

"11:45."

"It's only 11:00, Margaret."

"I know. I don't wanna miss it."

When I was in college and even many years later when I had moved out of town, I would arrive home to find Margaret sitting in the driveway or on the porch, waiting.

"How long have you been out here?" I'd ask.

Her reply was always the same, "Not very long."

Mama would tell me later that she had gone outside as soon as I called and said I was on my way. It could have been anywhere from thirty minutes to two hours before I would arrive. Margaret still waited.

I don't know if she has no concept of time or if she just doesn't want to miss anything. Mama says it's the latter—she says Margaret has a concept of everything.

On a trip to the beach for Mama's eighty-fourth birthday, we decided to play cards one night, so my friend and I taught Margaret how to play spades. Before we knew it, she had trumped somebody on all three hands with the ace. After laughing over

Margaret's uncanny ability to learn any new game, I remarked that I was tired.

"Embry, it's not time to go to bed," Margaret stated.

"That's 'cause you don't know when it's time to go to bed," Mama interjected.

Oh great, I thought. *Here we go.*

For years, the routine's been the same. Margaret talks on the phone until 9:00. Then, she sits at the computer playing solitaire while the TV blares her favorite show in the next room.

Mama sits on the couch reading a magazine or doing the crossword puzzle. Every now and then she'll holler an order at Margaret.

"Margaret, either come in here and watch this TV or turn it off."

At 11:00, they move into Mama's room where they watch the news together. At 11:30, Mama turns out the light and Margaret goes to her room. Evidently, the routine had changed just before we made this trip.

"I have to get up at 6:59 on Monday morning," Margaret announced from the back seat on our way home.

"What for?" I said.

"I'm going strawberry picking."

"Why are you gettin' up at 6:59?" I asked, chuckling.

"Embry, I have to get up before 7:00 because the van is picking me up at 8:30."

Then, Mama chimed in. "Margaret's been sitting up every night lately reading that calendar and looking at the CVS and Wal-Mart ads. I don't know how she's gonna get up at 7:00."

"Mama, I don't read Wal-Mart."

"What are you reading then?"

"K-Mart."

"Well, I still don't know how you're gonna get up," Mama added. "That light stays on until 12:00 every night."

"Mama, I don't stay up until 12:00," Margaret whined.

"Phooey," Mama replied.

"Mama, I don't."
"Well, what time do you stay up to then?"
Margaret gave Mama a serious look and said, "11:59."

Yelling and Spinning

"WE'RE HAVING A FREE SCREENING AT the clinic next month," I said to Mama. "Y'all need to come over and get your hearing checked. Hasn't Margaret been complaining about ringing in her ears?"

"Yeah, she has," Mama replied. "And I know I need to get mine checked. Sometimes, I can't hear a thing."

"Margaret must not be able to hear anything either," I said. "That TV's turned up so loud it could wake the dead."

"You think it's loud?" Mama asked.

"Just put it on your calendar," I said. "September twenty-ninth, that's a Monday. And why don't y'all plan to spend the night."

I knew that would get Margaret's attention. She loves to spend the night away from home. Mostly because there's a chance she can go out to eat, but also because she can use her "travel bag." A small bag stuffed full of hotel-sized shampoos, soaps and lotions; it stays packed at all times so she can leave on a moment's notice. Years ago, she wrote me a letter that read: *Embry, when can I come spin the night with you?* Margaret's always ready to "spin the night."

I walked into Margaret's room to tell her the good news. "Do you think you can find time in your busy schedule to come to

Auburn and spend the night?"

"What day?" she asked.

"It's on a Monday," I said. "I want you to come to the clinic and get your hearing checked."

"I have to go walk at Lake Bottom Park every Monday morning," she said, carefully perusing her calendar. "Then I have Sport Day on Tuesday."

"You can still make it to the park," I said. "Y'all don't need to be in Auburn until noon."

"Oh, okay," she said, still peering at the calendar. "But I have Bocce on Tuesday at 1:30. Do you think I'll make it back in time for that?"

"I'm not sure," I replied. "I guess it depends on whether or not you want to go out to lunch with me."

She took out her pen and wrote "no" next to Bocce on the calendar. "I can skip Bocce that week."

On the twenty-ninth, they made the forty-five-minute trip from Columbus to Auburn. The speech and hearing clinic is in the middle of campus and parking can be difficult. I had them meet me at my house and we drove over together.

When we got there, I filled out all the necessary paperwork, got Mama and Margaret to sign in the appropriate places and sat them down in the lobby—in the first two chairs next to the registration table. I wanted to make sure they would hear their names being called.

When I caught up with them an hour or so later, Dr. Krishnamurti, an audiology professor, and two graduate students were chatting with them about the results of their tests.

"Can you describe what kind of dizziness you're having?" he asked Margaret as I walked into the room.

"Sometimes the room spins around," she said, waving her hands above her head.

"I think they both need to come back for a full evaluation," he replied with a serious look on his face.

"I'm concerned about the ringing in Margaret's ears as well as the spinning. That's what she calls it," he said, winking at

Margaret. "I think she knows what she's talking about, though; she seems to be giving an accurate description."

"She's pretty good at telling you what's wrong," I said. "Margaret rarely complains about anything, so when she does, we take it seriously."

I picked up the cards their test results were written on. "This doesn't look good," I said, looking at Dr. Krishnamurti who was shaking his head.

"Your mother is only hearing at one frequency in both ears. She's not hearing anything at those higher frequencies."

"Nothing?" I said. "How in the world has she managed up until now?"

He shook his head. "I don't know, but I really think she could benefit from hearing aids."

"I don't understand it," I said. "They both seem to hear pretty well, considering."

"Well," he continued, "Margaret's not hearing anything at all in her left ear. That's the one she says is singing. I think we should investigate that further."

He looked at Mama and said, "You need to start mentally preparing yourself for hearing aids."

Mama shrugged her shoulders and nodded her head.

She hasn't heard a word he said, I thought to myself.

"I'll talk to her about it," I said, patting him on the shoulder.

"It's a good thing there's just the two of them, ha?" I laughed. "No one else would be able to deal with the loudness level in that house."

"I can tell they have a special bond," Dr. Krishnamurti said, smiling. "It seems they also have a unique way of communicating with each other."

"They do indeed," I said. "It's called yelling."

Daddy's Girl

MARGARET'S SMARTER THAN MOST PEOPLE THINK. She keeps it to herself, though; none of that spouting off at the mouth about all the things she knows. Anyway, Daddy always said, "It's better to be thought a fool than to open one's mouth and remove all doubt"—Margaret took heed.

Daddy was at liberty to just have fun with Margaret, with all of us for that matter. Mama did most of the parenting; she was in charge of discipline. Daddy was usually at work when we (more specifically, I) was being punished, although he could be counted on to give a follow-up spanking when he got home if Mama thought one was in order.

When Daddy was at home, he was off-limits. On a daily basis we'd hear Mama say, "Don't bother your daddy." Another reason why he rarely doled out punishment.

On most any night, if Daddy wasn't in his room watching television, you could find him in the living room, sitting in his favorite chair, listening to classical music. Holding a small piece of wood he had fashioned into a baton, he sat with his eyes closed, head back, and both arms thrusting into the air. He was not to be interrupted when he was conducting his imaginary symphony.

Daddy wasn't unapproachable at all. He was really just a big teddy bear. I always went to him first if the request was important. At least there was a chance of hearing "yes" as an answer, even if it was only temporary. The problem was he added a disclaimer: *It's fine with me, but go ask your mama.* Like I said, Mama did most of the parenting.

Every now and then, out of the blue, Margaret will tell someone she has a nickname, and that Daddy gave it to her. And every now and then, also out of the blue, I'll hear her say, "I miss Daddy."

Margaret learned a lot from Daddy. He was smart as a whip and funny. He loved to share jokes and was a wonderful storyteller. Margaret sat back and took it all in. She's smarter than most people think.

When I told Margaret I was writing a book about her, she had an interesting reply.

"What are you writing it about, all my Christmas lists?"

"Well yeah," I replied with a laugh, "those and a few other things."

"Who have you shown it to?" she asked.

"Oh, just a few people," I responded.

Several people have asked me if Margaret knows I'm writing a book about her. After pondering her response when I told her, I realized that Margaret exemplifies the perfect combination of innocence and brilliance. No unnecessary information hangs around in Margaret's head. She keeps what she needs and discards the rest.

My theory regarding her smarts was proven true recently when she had a minor surgical procedure performed on her eye. For some reason, the lashes on her upper eyelid had turned in and were scratching her eyeball. The ophthalmologist said they had to be removed and he would laser them off.

After the surgery, Mama called to tell me how Margaret was doing. She couldn't reach me at home so she left a message on my cell phone.

"I just wanted to tell you that everything went well and Margaret's doing fine. She hasn't been in any pain and says she can see better already."

She chuckled and said, "Oh, and one more thing. I thought you might like to hear this. Just as the doctor was about to put the needle in her eye to deaden it, Margaret looked up at him and said, 'Have you ever done this before?'"

Margaret's smarter than most people think.

Loaves and Fish

MY FRIENDS KNOW—IF MAMA INVITES you to stay and eat, you'll get full, but you're not going to understand how it happened.

"Don't you want something else?" Mama asks.

"No thanks," you say, "I'm full." The truth is, you only *think* you're full. She tricks you into it with lots of little bitty portions.

Most people go over board when they have company, not Mama. First, she has to make sure that Margaret doesn't have a chance to indulge on the leftover food, and then, there's the fact that she grew up during the Depression. She's not about to waste anything.

"Fold that tinfoil back up now, and put it over there on the counter," she says as I unwrap my baked potato.

"Mama, it's so thin, you can almost see through it."

"That doesn't matter," she says. "I can use it again."

"There's aluminum foil in this kitchen that's been here since the Depression," I say under my breath.

After we finish eating, there are two spoonfuls of corn left.

"Mama, do you want to save this corn?" I ask, knowing the answer before I even ask the question. "There's not much left."

"I wish you'd finish it," she says.

"I can't, Mama. I'm full."

"Well, put it in something. Margaret and I'll have it tomorrow."

I shake my head as I pour the corn into a small glass dish she uses specifically for the purpose of saving a leftover that wouldn't fill up a squirrel. But somehow, like the true miracle-worker himself, Mama can figure out a way to feed a multitude on very little. She'll take that little bitty dish out of the refrigerator for the next six days, dividing it up between her and Margaret each time.

My friends know and now they joke about it. "If you're going to eat at Augusta's house, you better eat before you go."

I'm glad they know; then they're not surprised when they sit down to several little dishes with only a smidgen of food in them.

It really is amazing how Mama can divide three ounces of squash between four people. And even more amazing that she'll keep pushing food at you until you say you've had enough when you're really thinking, *I haven't eaten a darn thing.*

Non-Sibling Rivalry

DEBBIE SULLIVAN MOVED TO COLUMBUS FROM California in 1986. Her father was retired and had remarried after her mother died of cancer. He and his new wife decided to return to Columbus as it was his boyhood home. Debbie and Margaret met through the recreation department and became best friends almost right away.

Debbie's stepmother, Dori, is a sweet, fun person who is a bundle of energy. She organized programs for people with disabilities in California, which is how she met Debbie and her father, Bill. When they moved to Columbus, Dori immediately sought out a place for Debbie to socialize. She found out about the bowling league and signed Debbie up. That's where Margaret entered the picture.

After a few weeks of checking out all the adults in the bowling league, Dori decided that Margaret would be the perfect best friend for Debbie. She literally picked Margaret out of the crowd and started inviting her to do things with them. When Mama told me this, I immediately thought of all those arranged marriages that end up in disaster. Luckily, Margaret and Debbie hit it off and have been friends for almost fifteen years—but then again, they never had to live together.

Debbie provided a perfect sibling rivalry that Margaret never had with me. From the start, they competed at everything. They bowled against each other, swam against each other and spent weekends together trying to beat each other at *Uno*.

If I happened to be at Mama's house when Debbie came to visit, I was constantly entertained with their bantering.

"Oh, Embry," Debbie said, "I just wanted to tell you that I bowled a 140 on Thursday."

"That's great, Debbie," I replied.

She directed her gaze across the room. "What was your score on Thursday, Margaret?"

Margaret sat staring at the television, acting like she couldn't hear.

"Margaret?" Debbie said again.

"I bowled a 126," Margaret mumbled under her breath.

"Oh," Debbie said, giggling.

According to Dori, Margaret was the one who inspired Debbie to learn how to swim. Debbie had a pool in her back yard, but she wouldn't do anything but hang onto the side and kick. When Margaret came to visit, she jumped in and started swimming. She made it look so easy and fun, Debbie had to give it a try.

Dori was smart; she picked Margaret for a reason. She knew that Margaret could do anything and would motivate Debbie. What she didn't know was that underneath Debbie's meek exterior was a competitor just dying to get out. Within a few months of learning how to swim, Debbie was challenging Margaret at the Special Olympics. Our local newspaper did a story about the two of them and their unique friendship. The picture was adorable—two smiling friends with medals around their necks and arms around each other.

Debbie and Margaret spent a lot of weekends together, either at our house or at Debbie's. The competition never let up. If Debbie was visiting when the Braves were playing, she would always cheer for the other team.

"Let's go Braves!" Margaret shouted.

"Let's go Mets!" echoed Debbie.

"I don't want the Mets, Debbie. I want the Braves."

Margaret's serious about the Braves. She was a good sport most of the time, but when it came to the Braves, her patience wore thin. If the Braves lost the game, Margaret blamed it on Debbie. They got mad, but then got over it—perfect best friends.

A few years ago, Debbie's family moved to Ocala, Florida. The separation was difficult for both of them, so now they visit each other a couple of times a year. Even though Margaret and Debbie don't get to see each other as often, they e-mail, talk on the phone and send each other cards and letters.

The competition continues, though, even long distance. Debbie calls to tell Margaret that she won a bowling tournament or Margaret sends an e-mail to say she won a gold medal in table tennis at the Georgia State Special Olympics. Just like sisters, best friends or both, Margaret will always have Debbie to keep her on her toes.

Margaret likes to win, but she's not obsessed with it. Anyway, she knows she's good, but modest, she's not.

"Margaret, who's the better bowler, you or Debbie?"

"Me."

"Who's the better swimmer?"

"Me."

I thought I'd have a little fun. "Who's the best sister?"

Smiling, she said, "Embry, you're my only sister."

Ladies Activity Club

DEBBIE'S STEPMOTHER DORI IS A MOVER and a shaker. When she gets an idea in her head, she's going to find a way to make it happen. The idea was that Margaret, Debbie and several of their friends needed to have a girls' night out.

Loretta Flowers, who started the bowling league, also organized a get-together one Friday night each month for members of the T.R. program in Columbus. Gathering at the Open Door Community Center, they would dance, watch movies, make crafts or play games, and, of course, they would eat—food was always the main attraction. Margaret and Debbie went to Open Door every time the door was open and had a grand time.

After almost a year, Loretta got pregnant and left the recreation department. Someone else was put in charge of the community center and according to Dori, it wasn't a safe environment. That's when she took over. Dori contacted someone at her church and asked if she could use their facility to keep the Friday night festivities alive. The church said yes and the Ladies Activity Club was born.

Drawing on her years of organizing programs in California, Dori created a wonderful, "real-life" experience for the members of the club. The ladies were required to dress (and did they ever), collect dues and record minutes. Dori taught them how to

138

conduct a formal business meeting and explained the duties of historian, secretary and treasurer. The most important thing was that the ladies had a chance to voice their opinions and exercise their independence, an invaluable experience.

Several of Dori's friends volunteered to lend their talents in the areas of flower arranging, makeup, proper dinner etiquette and the like. The ladies had talent shows, ethnic dinners and learned a lot of valuable skills. Margaret looked forward to it mostly because she got to dress up, but also because she got the chance to socialize with her best buddies. Then, of course, there was the food. According to Dori, the biggest hit was "Italian Night," when they had a huge Italian feast and even played an improvised game of Bocce.

"Really, though," Dori said, "the most wonderful thing about the Ladies Club was that the ladies shared something with the group each time we met. I was amazed at the insightful things they said and the topics that were discussed."

It was at the Friday night meeting that Margaret shared with her group of friends that Mama had been diagnosed with breast cancer.

"I was shocked," Dori said. "I had no idea that your mother had even been to see the doctor and then Margaret told us that!"

"Was she upset?" I asked.

"No, she was very calm and collected," Dori said. "But you know Margaret; she's strong, just like your mother. Those two are quite a pair."

Lost as $400

EVEN THOUGH MAMA'S OLD, SHE CERTAINLY doesn't look it. Then again, keeping up with Margaret is her secret to staying young. Everyone in our family looks younger than their age, even though Margaret has a subtle way of reminding us all how old we are—especially me.

For my fortieth birthday, the card from Margaret read:

> *Roses are red,*
> *Violets are blue,*
> *Happy Birthday,*
> *I love you.*
> *So much special.*

Then at the very bottom, an afterthought.

> *Embry P.S. Happy 40th Old Laidey.*

Even with Margaret's constant reminders for me and Mama, it's still hard for me to comprehend that my mama is old.

One evening, I answered the phone at her house. Expecting to hear someone asking for Margaret, I was surprised when I heard a solicitor's greeting.

"Yes, good evening, ma'am, may I speak with Mrs. Augusta Burrus?" the well-trained robot asked.

"This is her daughter," I said. "What can I do for you?"

"Oh, yes, ma'am," the voice continued. "I'm with the such and such company and I'd like to talk with Mrs. Burrus about life insurance. Is she available?"

"No, I'm sorry she's not."

"Well, ma'am, does she have life insurance?"

"Of course she does," I said. "She's eighty-four years old."

"Well, if I could just speak with her please," he interrupts.

"She can't come to the phone. And listen, please don't call this number again. My mother is an elderly woman and these calls really upset her."

As soon as I said it, I felt myself getting sweaty. I knew the poor, unsuspecting robot on the other end pictured a frail, bent-over, decrepit old lady.

"Okay, ma'am," he said. "I'm very sorry. You have a good evening."

"Thank you and same to you," I said. "Good-bye."

She's usually not interested, but Mama inquires after this caller. "Who was that?" she asks.

"Some solicitor, trying to sell you life insurance."

"Why'd you keep talking to him? I just say no thank you and hang up."

"Mama, if you do that, they'll just call back another night."

"Well, what did you say to him?"

"I told him not to call here anymore. That you're old and frail and those calls upset you."

Mama shakes her head and laughs, then I laugh too.

"Well, I am old," she says.

"Yeah, but not frail," I reply.

And frail, she's not. Mama piddles around in the yard every day, drives Margaret all over town, and plays soccer and baseball with her four-year-old grandson. And then there are the weekly trips to the YMCA. While Margaret does water aerobics, Mama walks on the treadmill—2.5 miles per hour for thirty minutes.

141

And no one would ever describe her as decrepit. She's five feet eight inches tall, although now she's shrunk to about five feet seven, is slim, trim and the picture of health for someone ten years younger. Not bad for a bent-over, frail, decrepit old woman.

The only thing that gives away Mama's age is her stories. Like the one she tells about "Mammy," the daughter of a slave who raised Mama and her three younger sisters. Mammy, whose real name was Ellen Waymire, came to Georgia from Virginia with her mother sometime in the late 1800s.

Mammy was the 1930s equivalent of a modern-day nanny. She lived in a small house behind the family's home and did everything from getting the children dressed every morning to showing them how to ring a chicken's neck.

"Mammy sat on the front porch and ruled the roost," Mama said, as her southern drawl got even thicker. "We sho had to mind our p's and q's around Mammy. She was tough, but we were crazy about her."

Stories and sayings, those are the things that give away Mama's age. She and Daddy both had sayings that no one born after 1930 would have ever heard. When they were growing up, Buffalo nickels were in circulation. A Buffalo nickel has an American Buffalo on one side and a Native American on the other. Anytime Daddy thought Mama was being too frugal, he'd recite his favorite line, "Your mama could squeeze a nickel till the Indian rides the buffalo."

Propped against the refrigerator door at her house, I observed Mama performing what appeared to be a ritual of some sort: She walked into the kitchen, out of the kitchen and then back in again within a period of five seconds.

"What's going on, Mama?"

"I can't remember what I came in here for," she said. "I swear, I'm as lost as $400."

"I've never heard that one before," I replied, chuckling.

Leaving the room again, she responded, "Well, can you find $400?"

142

Slinky Rooster

MARGARET LOVES BIRTHDAYS, NOT JUST HER own,
anybody's. Mama, on the other hand, can't stand birthdays.
Maybe it's because she's had more than just about anybody she
knows. I tell her constantly how young she looks, that no one
would ever know she's in her eighties. Her response is always the
same.

"I know what I look like."

"What?" I say.

"An old lady."

Margaret doesn't worry about getting old. Birthdays don't
signify aging to her anyway. They mean celebration, and any cause
to celebrate makes Margaret happy.

"My birthday's coming up, Embry."

"Margaret, it's October. Your birthday isn't until January."

"It's still coming up."

She makes her birthday list around the same time she makes
her Christmas list. Over the years, she's realized that if she
doesn't get something for Christmas, it can easily be worked onto
the birthday list. She even saves paper—years of exposure to
Mama's frugality have rubbed off on her—front, Christmas list,
back, birthday list.

For years, to celebrate Margaret's birthday, our family has

gotten together to have dinner at the restaurant of her choice. The evening includes, but is not limited to, Margaret dressing up in something shiny and Mama giving the pre-birthday dinner lecture.

"Now, Margaret, don't you tell those people it's your birthday, and don't order the biggest thing on the menu."

"Ugh, Mama, why not?"

"I don't want them coming over to our table doing all that singing and carrying on."

"But, Mama, you get free dessert."

"I don't care what you get, don't do it. Anyway, you can eat cake at home."

Over the years, Margaret's all but given up on achieving celebrity birthday status at a restaurant. There's no chance Mama's giving in.

Nobody told my sister-in-law the rules, though, or if somebody did, she decided to take matters into her own hands.

We all gathered at Red Lobster for Margaret's special day. The hostess directed us to a table in the corner. When given a choice, Mama always chooses a table that's out of the way. She doesn't want to sit in the middle of the restaurant in front of God and everybody calling attention to herself.

One by one, we climbed into the booth. Margaret sat on one side of me and Julie sat on the other. After we got our drinks, Julie looked at me and smiled. "I'll be back in a minute."

Soon she was back and we sat making small talk. Our food arrived and we all dug in.

Suddenly, what was a calm, quiet meal was interrupted by a loud noise. I looked up to see a group of smiling, clapping waiters and waitresses heading right for our table. I looked at Mama. She looked at Margaret, then at me.

"I didn't do it, Julie did!" I said as I looked at my sister-in-law and gave her a smile that said: "You go, girl!"

Margaret and little Jake clapped along. My brother, sister-in-law and I looked at each other and laughed. Mama's face was red. She had that look that said she wished the floor would open up and suck her in.

Then, just like that, they were gone, off to the next table of birthday revelers. No cake, no ice cream, nothing. Just clapping and loud singing. We looked at each other wondering where the reward was for Mama's humiliation.

After we recovered from the excitement, well disappointment, Margaret wanted to open her cards. Jake gave her one from him and Julie. "You're gonna love this one," he said, looking at me. My brother and I have always tried to one-up each other with witty cards.

Margaret, peering over her glasses, opened and closed the card several times, reading the front, then the inside.

"Do you know what it says, Marg?" my brother said, smiling and winking at me.

Margaret moved it closer, her head cocked, one eye an inch from the card, a bird-like stare.

"Let me see if I can make it out... Slinky...Rooster," she announced as if she'd just figured out the Pythagorean theorem.

Jake laughed so hard he almost knocked over his iced tea.

"Let me see that," I said, taking the card from Margaret.

On the front of the card were two pencil drawings. One was a spring, like the spring in a mattress, and next to it, a chicken. I opened it—inside, it said: *You Ain't.*

The spring really did look like a slinky, and the chicken, well, it could have been mistaken for a rooster, especially if you don't see chickens and roosters on a regular basis.

Jake was bent over the table. He tried to explain the card to Margaret through heaving breaths of laughter. "That's a spring and a chicken. Spring chicken."

"Oh," she said, as if she was really thinking, *Big deal.*

"Do you know what a spring chicken is?"

"Yes, I do."

Margaret never just says yes or no. She always adds something.

"What?" Jake said, still laughing.

"A chicken."

Even though the punch was gone, with the new translation, we all thought it was the funniest card we'd ever seen.

As we sat around talking about birthdays, Margaret reminded us all that Jake had turned fifty-four in December.

"I know, Marg. I'm gettin' old," he sighed.

I couldn't resist. "Yeah, Jake, slinky rooster, you ain't!"

Baseball Fever

MARGARET KNOWS THE NAMES OF ALL the players on the Atlanta Braves baseball team. She also knows the coaches and the bat boys, probably even the maintenance people.

When I told her that my friend, Amy Richter, who worked for the Braves, invited her to spend a day at the ballpark, I expected excitement, elation, hands clapping, feet stomping. Instead, she gave me a serious look.

"Will I get to meet Bobby Cox?"

"Margaret, he's the manager of the team. He'll be too busy."

"Not before the game he won't."

About that time, Mama chimed in. "Now, Margaret, beggars can't be choosers."

"Mama, I'm not begging."

"Well, don't ask for anything. Embry's friend sure is nice to do this for you. Now you just go and have a good time. And don't forget to say thank you!"

"I won't, Mama."

Margaret got dressed in her Braves T-shirt and off we went to Atlanta.

We arrived two hours before the game started. Amy met us on the concourse and led us to her office where she presented Margaret with a souvenir bag filled with all kinds of Braves goodies. Margaret rifled through and found a hat which she immediately plopped on her head. She looked up at me, grinning.

"I'm going to get the players to sign my hat."

I had brought a camera to record as many of the day's events as possible, but when we got to the field, Amy told us she had arranged for the Braves' official photographer to take pictures.

Margaret would receive a package several weeks later containing ten glossy photos and a signed team poster.

Down on the field, several players were talking with fans and media. Amy motioned for one of them to come over. A tall, handsome young man came striding toward us.

"Kenny, this is Margaret."

"Hey, Margaret, it's nice to meet you," he said.

"Margaret, this is Kenny."

"Your last name's Lofton," Margaret said, grinning from ear to ear.

"Yes, it is," he said, laughing.

Several other players came over and were introduced. They signed her hat, put their arms around her, smiled for the camera and made small talk. Lots of players, no Bobby Cox.

"Where's Bobby Cox?" Margaret asked Amy.

"He's meeting with the other coaches. He doesn't usually come out until the game's about to start."

About that time, Fred McGriff, one of Margaret's favorite players, walked up to say hello. She temporarily forgot about Bobby Cox.

The next stop was the *Coca-Cola Sky Field* where kids of all ages can see what it's like to run from home plate to first base on a real baseball field. Margaret put down all her souvenirs, paused at home plate for two seconds, then took off running to the base ninety feet away, her laughter filling the air. We drank Cokes and had our picture taken next to the forty-foot Coke bottle made out of bats, gloves, balls and a myriad of other baseball paraphernalia.

From there, Amy took us to the press box where you get a bird's-eye view of the game, as well as a chance to see the inner workings of the baseball world. I was amazed. Margaret couldn't have cared less, she wanted to see Bobby Cox.

Just as we were leaving, John Schuerholz, the Braves' general manager walked into the hall.

I was thinking, *What a treat for Margaret. He's the top guy, even better than Bobby Cox.* He stopped to say hello to Amy and she introduced us.

"John, I'd like you to meet my friend, Margaret."

"Hello, Margaret, it's nice to meet you," he said.

"John, I'm a Braves' fan all the way," Margaret said, shaking his hand.

He laughed. "I tell you what, Margaret, we need more fans like you."

As he turned to leave, Margaret stopped him.

"John, can I ask you something?"

"Sure," he said, smiling politely.

"Do you know Bobby Cox?"

Contraband

ONCE A MONTH, MARGARET'S T.R. GROUP goes on a trip. Alice French-Brewer, the group's fearless leader, organizes trips to various points of interest all around middle and South Georgia—strawberry picking in Reynolds, the Little White House in Warm Springs or the Aviation Museum in Warner Robbins.

Alice also started a Georgia history club so the T.R. group could learn more about their home state. Everywhere they go, they take pictures of monuments, historical markers or famous buildings—learning made fun. Some trips are planned in advance, others are just written on the monthly calendar under the heading, "Mystery Trip." Somehow, Margaret always knows where they're going, so the only real mystery is how much money she can coax out of Mama to take on the day-long outing.

Between garden club, history club and cooking class, Margaret's turned into a bona fide Renaissance woman.

"Did you know that the Cherokee rose is the Georgia state flower?" she said to me one day out of the blue.

Shocked, I replied, "No, I had no idea."

About a year ago, Alice started taking a group down to Biloxi, Mississippi. No mystery here, they went to gamble. After Alice explained to her how a slot machine worked, Margaret was thrilled. She couldn't wait to start pumping money into this Las

Vegas version of a vending machine.

The night before Margaret left on her first junket, Mama laid down the law.

"Now, Margaret, I don't want you putting anything bigger than a nickel in those slot machines."

Margaret didn't know enough about gambling to contest Mama.

"Well, I need a lot of nickels then," she said as she piled more clothes into her suitcase.

"And that's enough clothes," Mama said. "You're only gonna be there for two days."

Mama goes through Margaret's bag before she goes anywhere; she's a veritable clothes Gestapo. This time, Margaret got the jump on her and stashed away two shiny outfits, several pieces of costume jewelry and some makeup, the contents of her bag an indication that she had plans to spend her bounty.

Mama sifted through the bag and found the contraband.

"Margaret, why are you taking all these dressy clothes?"

"Alice said to bring one dressy outfit."

Alice is a true friend. She indulges Margaret's taste in gaudy clothes and jewelry, as well as her desire to get dressed up for a night on the town.

Mama countered. "Well, you've got two or three. You don't have any business haulin' all those clothes down there. Now take something out."

Dejected, Margaret took a sequin blouse and a pair of black pants out of the bag and laid them on the bed.

Satisfied, Mama left the room.

I winked at Margaret and put the contraband back into her bag. "This will be our secret, okay?"

She giggled. "Don't worry, Embry, I won't tell."

Three days later, Margaret arrived exhausted, her bag filled with nickels. "I won the jackpot!" she proudly said to Mama as she came in the door.

"I hope you won more than you lost," came Mama's reply.

"I won twenty-five dollars!" Margaret said.

"Well, that's good, but how much did you have to spend to win it?"

"Only a nickel."

"A nickel my foot," Mama muttered under her breath. "I bet you spent thirty dollars to win twenty-five."

"Mama, no I didn't."

Alice told Mama that Margaret's jackpot had paid 400 nickels and that everyone on the machines around her clapped and cheered. Sirens blared and lights flashed. Margaret had been on top of the world.

"You would have thought she'd won the lottery," Alice said, chuckling.

And as far as Margaret was concerned, she had.

Get Your Money

HAVE I MENTIONED THAT MARGARET CAN be sassy? Along with her sweetness comes a little hot sauce, but I guess that's to be expected. She has the right to get moody like the rest of us, doesn't she? After all, she's only human.

Her feistiness has raised its unexpected head on several occasions; during Special Olympics competitions, arguing her case with Mama and, sometimes, right out of the clear blue sky.

I walked into the den to find her scouring the pages of the phone book. "Whatcha looking for, Margaret?"

"I'm trying to find the number for Goodwill," she said, sounding agitated.

"Why are you looking under 'N'?" I asked, peering over her shoulder.

"'N' for 'industries,' Embry. It's called Goodwill Industries."

"Margaret, 'industries' starts with an 'I' not an 'N.' Anyway, you need to look under 'G' for Goodwill. If it's the name of a business, you look up the first name, not the second. I thought you knew that."

She glared at me and said, "Evidently I didn't."

I was struck dumb by her comeback and had absolutely no reply. I've been struck dumb more than once when it comes to Margaret and her antics. You never know what she's going to pull.

As we left church one day, Margaret spoke up from the back seat. "Where are we going for lunch?"

"We're going to eat lunch at home," Mama replied.

"Ugh, Mama, I don't wanna eat lunch at home."

"Why not?"

"Because I wanna go out to eat."

Winking at me, Mama looked at Margaret and said, "Do you have any money?"

"Yes, I do," Margaret replied.

"What do you wanna do for lunch?" Mama said, looking at me.

"Oh, I don't care," I said. "We can go out if Margaret wants to."

We went home to change clothes and as soon as we got in the door Mama said, "Alright, Margaret, if you wanna go out to eat, you better get your wallet."

Margaret disappeared into her room and emerged a few minutes later with a bulging fanny pack fastened securely around her waist. Margaret doesn't carry a purse, she wears a fanny pack and carries everything she owns in it. Because they get so much wear, she's gone through at least a dozen in the past five years.

"I'm ready," Margaret said, heading for the door.

At the restaurant, Mama looked directly at Margaret and recited the standard restaurant operating procedure: *Don't order the biggest thing on the menu.*

While Margaret figured out what she wanted to eat, I picked up her fanny pack. I was dying to know what she had crammed in there to make it so full.

"Margaret, you must have a lot of money in here," I said. "This thing's heavy."

Margaret stared at the menu, not saying a word. I pulled out a camera, some makeup, a wad of Kleenex, her wallet, and a copy of her monthly schedule, folded into a neat little square.

"Lord, Margaret, you've got everything but the kitchen sink in here."

Mama smiled and said, "How much money did you bring, Margaret?"

Margaret acted like she didn't hear.

"Margaret!" Mama said again, only louder.

"What?"

"How much money did you bring?

"I didn't bring any money."

"Didn't bring any money?" Mama said. "I told you to get your money."

"Mama, you didn't tell me to get any money. You told me to get my wallet."

Walking to Jerusalem

MARGARET NEVER ADMITS WHEN SHE'S SICK. As a matter of fact, she'll deny it until the cows come home. And if you keep on about it, she gets adamant.

"Margaret, you sound terrible, are you sick?"

"No, I'm not sick."

"Well, you sure do sound like it."

"Embry, I'm not sick. And I won't be sick on Friday either because I have to go to a dance at the Comer Auditorium."

Margaret's perpetual denial of the obvious and "never say die" attitude must be a family trait. Based on what I know about our maternal grandmother and great-grandmother, I'd say she comes by it honestly. I don't even think it skipped a generation.

"Where did my name come from?" I asked Mama sometime during my elementary school years.

"Well, you were named after me, but I was named after your great-grandmother. 'Embry' was her maiden name."

"Oh, what was she like?" I asked in hopeful anticipation. I was tired of being teased about my name. I just knew this namesake, whoever she was, was going to make it all worthwhile.

"Well, I never knew her because she died before I was born," Mama said. "But I always thought she must have been the meanest woman in the world."

Just what I wanted to hear. "How was she mean?" I asked.

"Well, she just didn't put up with any kind of foolishness," Mama said. "People used to tell me all the time, 'Your grandmother wouldn't have liked that, or 'Your grandmother wouldn't have let you wear those pants.' One of our neighbors used to tell me almost every day, 'Your grandmother would've had a fit if she'd seen you in those overalls.'"

"She sounds scary," I replied.

"I don't know if she really was or not," Mama said. "But I heard so many stories about her, I decided that she must have been horrible. If she *had* known me, I'm sure she would've been on me like nobody's business."

So see, Margaret really can't help it, even her great-grandmother was a no-nonsense kind of person. The meanest woman in the world obviously passed that stubborn gene on to her daughter, who was our grandmother, Mamie.

Mamie's real name was Mabel Pearce Andrews. The reason we called her Mamie was because that's what came out when Mama's first cousin, George, tried to say "Aunt Mabel."

"All of our friends and relatives thought that was grand," Mama said. "So everybody started calling her Mamie, including Katharine, Isabel and me, her own children."

Mamie was a devout Southern Baptist and never missed a Sunday service; she was practically in church every time the doors opened. She even traveled to the Holy Land in her late seventies and nearly expired when the bus she was traveling on broke down in the desert.

"I can't believe Mamie survived that trip," I responded after Mama told me what happened.

"You don't know Mamie then," Mama said. "She would have walked the rest of the way to Jerusalem if she'd had to. She wasn't about to let a bus breaking down keep her from getting to the Holy Land."

"I guess Mamie thinks you're not going to heaven if you don't go to church every Sunday, huh?"

Mama laughed. "Mamie thinks you're not going to heaven if

you don't go to the First Baptist church every Sunday."

"Well, I'm sure she thinks I'm a heathen. When and if I do go to church, it's not the same one she goes to."

"She doesn't think you're a heathen," Mama said. "Just a Presbyterian."

Like Margaret, Mamie would never admit if she wasn't feeling well. In all of her ninety-one years, she gave in only once. A pain in her stomach turned out to be gallstones and she had to be hospitalized. According to Mama, she caused quite a ruckus and had the hospital staff steppin' and fetchin'.

A young, green nurse came into Mamie's room to administer her medication. As the story goes, Mamie sat straight up in bed, waved her finger in the girl's face and said in her most ladylike tone, "I'm not taking that."

"Why not?" the nurse responded.

"Because I'm not sick," Mamie said. "You need to take that medicine down the hall and give it to somebody who needs it."

Turtle Lady

ONE YEAR, ALICE TOOK SEVERAL MEMBERS of Margaret's T.R. group to Cape San Blas, a remote beach in Northwest Florida. One of her former professors from Columbus State University owns a vacation home there and he offered it to Alice for the weekend. Cape San Blas is one of the last frontier beaches in Florida; no hotels, no restaurants and not many people, just a quiet place for fishing, swimming and shelling.

When Alice told the group where they were going, Margaret just about did a backflip. The beach is her favorite place on earth. She began packing that very night even though the trip was a week away. With Mama standing guard, Margaret packed several outfits (at least two shiny ones), two bathing suits, her fancy new "beach dress," beach shoes, beach towel and of course, her camera.

Finally the day came, and at 7:00 in the morning, they all piled into the van and headed south to Florida. Usually, the group sings or plays games along the way. This time, Alice told everyone to call out anything they saw related to farming, nature or flowers. As they left Georgia and drove into the Alabama countryside, the competition got heated.

"Cow!" a voice shouted from the back.

"Barn!" another voice chimed in.

After a few minutes of silence, someone in the very back yelled, "Hey!"

"What?" Alice yelled back, almost running off the road.

"Hey!" the voice demanded.

"Hey!" Alice replied.

From the back again came, "Hey, hey, hey!"

"What's all that heying about?" Alice finally said, looking in the rearview mirror.

"It's hay, Alice. I see some hay," said Margaret from her seat in the back.

After five hours of driving, they arrived at Shadowfax, their home for the weekend. A few dark clouds and rain threatened the skies, but their spirits were not dampened. Most of them were chomping at the bit to get in the water, so Alice's sister Mary Anna, who came along to help, took a group down to the beach before lunch.

As the story goes, Margaret was decked out in her bathing suit, beach dress (a name she gave her bathing suit cover-up) and newly purchased "beach shoes." She always has to look the part, no matter what the occasion. She put down her towel, took off her glasses, shoes and cover-up and splashed into the surf.

Within minutes, a strong storm blew up and someone noticed Margaret's stuff flying down the beach. Scrambling out of the water, Margaret took off after her things. The cover-up was all she found, though; everything else was gone with the wind.

Mary Anna sent everyone back to the house and she and Margaret set off down the beach in search of the missing loot— most important of which were her glasses.

Margaret can't see anything without her glasses. Her lenses are so powerful, if you hold them up to the sun at just the right angle, you could start a fire on a hot, dry day. They had to find those glasses.

She and Mary Anna walked almost a mile down the beach, but to no avail. Dejected, Margaret stomped back to the house. Alice was fixing lunch when they walked in.

"Did you find them?" Alice asked.

"No and Mama's gonna kill me," Margaret whimpered.

"Don't worry, Margaret. If we don't find 'em, I'll explain everything to your mama," Alice replied in her most reassuring voice.

"Tomorrow, we'll ask the lady who drives the turtle cart if she found them. She drives around in a golf cart and picks up everything people leave on the beach."

The next day, the whole group went out in search of the turtle cart. Sure enough, the turtle lady said her neighbor had found some towels and shoes and had left them in a remote area of the beach several miles down.

"Did he find any glasses?" Mary Anna asked.

"No, he didn't say anything about glasses," the turtle lady replied.

Margaret was really upset now. Despite the fact that she couldn't see her hand in front of her face, she was more worried about having to explain the lost glasses to Mama when she got home.

When they got to the cove the turtle lady told them about, they found all of Margaret's things—shoes, towel and, believe it or not, even those glasses.

Whoever found those glasses knew that someone was missing them in the worst way. I imagined Margaret's guardian angel picking them up, peering through the lens, swooning from a dizzy spell and falling over in the sand.

The guardian angel had placed them on top of a piece of driftwood as if they were on display in an eyeglass store for beachcombers.

Mary Anna was the first one to see them. "Well, Margaret, looks like somebody's watching over you," she said, picking up the glasses and examining them for damage. Handing them to Margaret, she said, "I'm afraid the frames might be a little bent."

"My glasses!" Margaret shouted.

Lots of whooping and hollering from the group followed.

"Are they okay, Margaret?"

"Yes, they're fine," she said, carefully placing them on her face and pushing on the frames to make sure they were in just the right place. Margaret's constantly pushing on the frames so her glasses remain in a perpetual state of bent.

Once the glasses were safely back with their owner, everyone piled into the van and headed home to tell Alice the good news.

"I found 'em, Alice," Margaret yelled, bouncing up the steps to the house.

"See there, I told you everything would be all right," Alice said, giving her a big squeeze. "Tomorrow, we'll find the turtle cart lady and tell her to thank her neighbor for putting your stuff in a safe place."

"I think it's a miracle that somebody found those glasses," Mary Anna said, shaking her head.

"Yep," said Alice. "That's what I call divine intervention."

The rest of the group had gone out on the patio and Margaret was trailing behind. Alice and Mary Anna stood in the living room.

"I wonder who found them," Mary Anna said to Alice.

Margaret stopped at the door. "I know who found them," she casually replied.

"Who?" said Mary Anna, somewhat taken aback.

Margaret smiled and said, "You did."

Miss Georgia

MARGARET'S NEVER AT A LOSS FOR the right thing to say. Mama has her so well groomed, she could win a Miss Manners contest hands-down. She's even taught me a thing or two.

As we rode our bikes through the park, Margaret spotted a young woman who had been her coach at a Special Olympics swim meet.

"Hey, Laura," Margaret said, stopping her bike.

"Oh, hey, Margaret," Laura responded. "How are you?"

In her most professional voice, Margaret said, "Laura, I'd like you to meet my sister, Embry. Embry, this is Laura."

I was dumbfounded. *Where had she learned to make introductions like that?* Boy, Mama really had been busy.

The nuances of southern social etiquette aren't lost on Margaret either. She says "yes, ma'am" and "no, ma'am" and "nice to meet you." She has perfect phone manners. She knows where to put the dinner fork as well as the dessert fork. She knows how to write a thank-you note and even adds an extra touch. Margaret's notes go above and beyond polite: *Thank you for the _____ I will use it everyday.*

She pours it on good with me too, her own sister. She slides in next to me on the couch. "I love you, Embry. You're sweet, beautiful, gorgeous...Miss Georgia."

"Okay, Margaret," I say. "What do you want?"

She giggles and says, "I don't want anything."

And the truth of the matter is, she really doesn't, but she still knows how to turn on the old southern charm.

Over the years, my friends and I have had many discussions regarding the realities of our southern upbringing; the foremost being our mothers' desire to perpetuate through us the southern demeanor. You're taught to be polite, demure and passive—a sure-fire recipe for disaster.

As one of my friends so eloquently stated, "We spend the first twenty years of our lives learning to be genteel and the next twenty in therapy trying to erase it all. And you know what happens then, we just end up becoming passive-aggressive."

Yep, that southern gene is hard to stamp out—even in the case of someone as innocent and naïve as Margaret. I realized this one day when I called home to check in. I was quickly aware that I had interrupted a conversation when Margaret answered the phone.

"Hello?" she said, sounding very distressed.

"Hey, Marg, it's me."

In the background, I could hear Mama engaged in a full-fledged diatribe even though her sparring partner had obviously disengaged.

"What's Mama fussing about?" I said.

"I asked her if I could go to Biloxi with Alice."

"What, she said you couldn't go?"

"She said I don't need to go again because I already went one time."

"I'm sorry, Margaret. I know how much you like doing things with Alice."

Silence greeted me on the other end.

"Margaret, are you okay?"

"I'm okay," she said.

"You're not crying, are you?"

"No."

"Are you sure you're okay?"

After a brief pause, she said, "I know what I can say about Mama."

I couldn't wait to hear this one. "What?"

Margaret breathed a heavy sigh. "Mama's just hard to please."

Well, there you have it, I thought. Generations of southern women will spend countless hours and ridiculous amounts of money in search of the truth when Margaret, in her infinite wisdom, laid it out in five simple words.

Balancing Books

DON'T ASK MARGARET TO BALANCE A checkbook. She wouldn't have a clue about what to do with the numbers. Ask her to balance the numbers from her bowling scores, though, and she can do that in a flash. I know because I caught her in the act.

On a warm Saturday in August, I drove over to Columbus to watch Margaret bowl in a Master's bowling tournament sponsored by Special Olympics. I arrived to find the bowling alley packed to the gills with bowlers from all over the state of Georgia.

As I mentioned earlier, Margaret is serious about bowling. I had seen her bowl at least a dozen times in her weekly bowling league, but I had never seen her bowl in a tournament. I was about to find out just how serious she was.

Alice came up and greeted me when I got inside. "Hey, Embry. Margaret's over there on lane ten."

"Have you seen Mama?" I asked.

"Yeah, I saw her a few minutes ago but I don't know where she went."

"That's okay. I'll find her," I replied. "Hey, how's Margaret doing?"

"I don't know," Alice said. "They just got started."

About that time, Mama appeared out of the sea of faces. "Hey, dahlin'," she said, giving me a hug.

"Hey, Mama, have you seen Margaret yet?"

"Yeah, she's right over there." Mama pointed toward a crowd of bowlers dressed in matching shirts, chatting with each other.

We pushed our way through the mass of people until we stood close enough to see all the action. Margaret was decked out in full regalia—bowling shirt, bowling shoes and that thing that bowlers wear, some kind of glove I guess, on her left hand. As she waited for her turn, she wiped her ball over and over with the dirtiest towel I'd ever seen.

"When did Margaret start using all of those props?"

"Oh, she's had 'em a long time," Mama said. "And that towel is just horrible. She won't let me wash it; she says it's good luck."

"Boy, she is really into this, isn't she?"

"You don't know the half of it."

We watched for a while and then as Margaret stood up to bowl her last frame, I yelled, "Let's go, Margaret. I wanna see a strike!"

Margaret didn't flinch. She picked up the shiny purple ball, gave it one more rub with the good luck towel and marched to her position. We stood in hopeful anticipation as she lined up and flung the ball down the lane. When she saw she'd left three pins standing, she walked back to her seat, glanced up at the electronic scorekeeper, then got out a miniature notepad and scribbled down some numbers.

"What's she writing?"

"She writes down all of her scores in that book," Mama said.

I walked down to where Margaret was sitting to congratulate her on the game. She was poring over the notebook, still writing.

"Hey, Marg, how'd you do?"

"I bowled a 125," she said, sounding dejected.

I picked up the notebook and examined it closely. "Your notebook says 225."

I could tell that she had first written down "125," her correct score, but in the time it took me to walk down three steps, Margaret had worked some magic with her pen—the "1" was changed to a "2."

"I changed it," she said rather matter-of-factly.

"Why did you do that?"

"I just like to."

"Margaret, that's cheating," I said with a laugh. "You need to change that back."

"I don't have to change it, Embry. It's my book."

One Key

I NEVER CEASE TO BE AMAZED at the plethora of information available on the Internet. In doing research about Down syndrome, whether for work or personal reasons, I've found thousands of informative websites. The ones that really jumped out at me, though, were some that I came across simply by chance.

Hi, my name is so and so and I have Down syndrome. Please read on to learn more about me and all the things I've accomplished.

I'm always taken aback when I hear people with Down syndrome actually talk about Down syndrome, because my reference is my sister—a smart, loving, wonderful human being who couldn't tell you what Down syndrome was if you asked her. Margaret gets along just fine not knowing that the world sees only her limitations.

Ask anyone who knows her and they would describe Margaret as a high functioning person with Down syndrome. She's articulate, funny and sociable. My friends say she has a better social life than I do. Margaret's life is full, yet beautifully simple. As smart as she is, Margaret has no idea, nor does she need to know, that she is different from the rest of us.

Many years ago, Margaret got a job at a Goodwill thrift store. Every day for two years, she got up at the crack of dawn to get to work by 7:00 a.m. Not one day was she out because she was sick or had an appointment. Not once did she complain about how boring her job was or how little money she made. Not once would you hear her say, as so many people do, "I hate my job."

Now don't get me wrong—one of the reasons Margaret liked having a job is because she likes to spend money. She loves having money in her wallet, although she never knows how much she has. Spending money is her strong suit, understanding the value of it is not.

"Let's go out to lunch," she says to me. "I'll treat."

"Do you have enough money?" I respond.

"Yes, I've got three ones."

For several years before he died in 2001, Mama's Cousin George sent Margaret a check for $100 every month. The first check came completely unannounced one July. In the memo section it read: *For Summer Fun.*

Margaret looked at it and exclaimed, "Oooh, ten dollars!"

Ten dollars or a hundred dollars, it was all the same to her. Margaret doesn't understand wealth, social status or any other aspects of life the rest of us use to define ourselves. She doesn't care if your car is new or old. She doesn't care if you're fat or thin. She wouldn't even care if you'd been in jail. If she met you, she would love and accept you, no matter who you are.

A simple, wonderful life she lives—so simple, she only needs one key. That's right, just one key, stuck in the middle of fifteen souvenir key chains. Most of us have so many keys we can't keep up with them—keys to cars, homes and jobs. It seems that everything in our material lives requires locking and unlocking. But that's not the case for Margaret. The only key she needs is one that will open the front door of her house in the rare event that Mama's not home to open it for her.

That's when you know you have a simple life. When you're like Margaret and you only need one key.

Lucky

"MARGARET, WHAT'S JAKE'S CELL PHONE NUMBER?"

"Margaret, put milk and eggs on the grocery list."

"Margaret, what's that lady's name we saw in the mall the other day?"

Mama doesn't need a Palm Pilot—she has Margaret.

Margaret never forgets anybody's name or an appointment, and she knows where she and Mama are supposed to be at all times.

"Margaret, when are we supposed to go to Callaway?"

"Friday, the fifteenth."

Margaret and Mama volunteer at Callaway Gardens, a 14,000 acre resort and preserve in Pine Mountain, Georgia. Callaway Gardens is known for its beautiful lakes, gardens, and nature trails. One of its most fascinating attractions is the Day Butterfly Center, which is also Mama and Margaret's assigned post on volunteer day. Margaret can answer almost as many questions as Mama can about the various species of butterflies, but her main job is making sure the laminated butterfly guides, or menus, as Margaret calls them, don't walk out the door.

"I make sure everybody puts their menu in the outbox," she replied, when I asked her how she spends her Friday morning one day a month.

Even though Margaret's good at keeping up with menus and schedules, she doesn't always do well with messages. I found this out when I lived with them for about nine months while finishing graduate school. If the phone's not for her and she has to take a message, things get sticky. She has difficulty remembering whether the person will call back or whether you are supposed to call said person back. Luckily, the person leaving the message, no matter who it is, never gets upset when you tell them Margaret wrote it down wrong; even the orneriest of callers.

"Why didn't you call me back?" my demanding friend said to me.

"Margaret said you would call me back," I replied.

"Oh, well that's alright," he said. "That Margaret's a hoot, isn't she? She gave me your whole schedule—told me where you were, what you were doing, and what time you were supposed to be back."

"Yeah, she's a riot," I replied, thinking I would have a chat with Margaret when she got home.

When a group of people at Mama and Margaret's church decided to start a program for young people called *Logos*, Margaret was one of the first people they asked to help out. For four years, Margaret has spent her Wednesday afternoons volunteering her time at church. She does whatever is necessary and never complains about anything, no matter what the task.

At the end of the year banquet, Margaret Page, the organizer of the program, stood at the podium and thanked everyone who volunteered their time and talents. After she finished congratulating everyone, she said, "I have a special gift for my *Logos* angel. Margaret Burrus, will you come up here please?" Margaret Page continued saying, "I don't know what I would have done without Margaret." When Margaret got to the podium, she placed a shiny, handmade crown on her head. While Margaret grinned from ear to ear, everyone in the room clapped and a few even got teary-eyed, Mama included.

Margaret's gift of love reaches far past her immediate surroundings. For years, she insisted on sitting up all night to watch the Jerry Lewis Muscular Dystrophy Telethon. She drove Mama crazy to let her dial the number and call in a $25 pledge. Perched in front of the television in the den, Margaret would do her best to stay up all night, but without fail, Mama would find her sound asleep on the sofa the next morning.

Margaret also helps out at our nephew's preschool. Pauline Marth, whose mother was a good friend of Mama's, is the director of the school. She asked Mama if Margaret would like to volunteer one day a week as a teacher's aide. Touched by her kind gesture, I called Pauline to thank her.

"Your sister is just remarkable, Embry," she said.

"Yes, she is, isn't she?" I said, beaming.

"She's such a big help to me and the children just love her."

"Pauline, that was really sweet of you to think about Margaret and ask her to do this. I know she enjoys herself." I pictured Margaret standing at the easel covered with finger paint, a group of four-year-olds gathered around her.

"You don't have to thank me," Pauline said. "I'm just so glad she wanted to help out. She's certainly a special human being."

I felt the tears coming. "Yes, she is," I replied. "She's a blessing to our family—a true gift from God."

"You're lucky to have a sister like Margaret."

"I am," I said. "Just about the luckiest person in the world."

A Celebration of Life

"LET'S HAVE A BIG PARTY," MY sister-in-law whispered across the table. We were having Sunday lunch at my brother and sister-in-law's house. The conversation had turned to Mama's eighty-fifth birthday that was looming in the not so distant future.

I nodded my head and smiled. "Okay," I mouthed back, but I was really thinking, *I don't know how we're going to pull this off, Mama hates parties.*

A week or so later, Julie mentioned the party again when we talked on the phone.

"I don't know if she'll like that," I replied. "She's always told me she doesn't like parties. And she'll have a fit if she thinks we went to any trouble or expense."

"Well, then we won't tell her," she offered.

I was still reluctant. I agreed that a party was in order, but at the same time, I believed that we should honor Mama's wishes. Not many people make it to their eighty-fifth year of life, and even fewer make it that far in good health and with enough wits about them to tell you in no uncertain terms what they do and don't want.

"Well, okay," I said, "but let's not make it too big. I want her to enjoy it."

So it was settled, the party would be a surprise and for family

174

only—if Mama didn't know about it, at least she wouldn't spend the next several weeks telling us why she didn't need a party or how we needed to save our money for something important—the less fretting that went on, the better.

After tossing around a few ideas about where to have the big event, Julie decided that she and Jake would host the party at their house. They would handle the food and decorations and I was put in charge of contacting family members.

Over the next week, I made phone calls, wrote letters and sent e-mails. Family members from Montana to Washington, D.C., and south were invited. I knew everybody would want to know about Googa's eighty-fifth birthday party.

"Googa" is the name given to my mother by Bitsy, her oldest niece. Bitsy's first attempt to say "Aunt Augusta" came out "Googa," so Mama was introduced to all the nieces and nephews that followed by the funny name that Bitsy coined.

Once I had gotten confirmation from everyone who was coming, I debated over when I should tell Margaret. I knew how excited she would be about a party, but I decided to wait because I knew there was a good chance she'd blow the surprise. That's just how Margaret is; she can't help herself.

After lots of errand running and sewing up last-minute details, I drove to Columbus. I dropped the cake off at Jake and Julie's then headed to Mama's house to pick up Mama and Margaret and drive them to little Jake's soccer game. While we waited for Mama to get ready, I took Margaret outside and told her about the party. I explained how important it was for her to keep it a secret.

"You can't say a word about it," I instructed.

"I won't say anything," she whispered, shaking her head.

Okay, that's taken care of, I thought. *Now I just have to figure out a way to get over to Jake and Julie's this afternoon to help set up without raising any suspicion.*

After the soccer game, little Jake decided he wanted to ride home with us instead of going with my brother. He and Mama got in the back seat and Margaret and I piled into the front. Suddenly, Jake blurted out something about us coming over for dinner that night. Then, before I could do anything to stop it, Margaret added her two cents.

"Jake, I'm not supposed to say anything about tonight."

I calmly slid my index finger across my throat and things got worse.

"Embry, I'm not gonna say anything."

"Well then don't," I replied, shaking my head furiously.

Between Jake's loud talking and her hearing loss, Mama hadn't heard all of our conversation. I still wasn't sure that Margaret would stop talking, so I gestured wildly. This time she got the message.

Several people had plans or lived too far away to come to the party, but we still ended up with eleven guests plus the five members of our immediate family. The plan was for everyone to gather at Jake and Julie's house by 6:45, then, Mama, Margaret and I would arrive at 7:00.

Explaining that I needed to take little Jake home, I rushed over to help Julie get set up. I made the salad, set the table and buttered biscuits. When all was done, I rushed back home to take a shower and get dressed for the party. As I tried to relax under the hot water, my mind was filled with all the things that could still go wrong. I played the worst-case scenarios over in my head: *Margaret would blab, Mama would recognize my aunts' and uncle's cars, or worst of all, nobody would be there when we arrived.*

We finished getting ready and I ushered Mama and Margaret into the car. After a five-minute trip, we pulled up to what appeared to be an empty house—no cars parked in front of the house or in the driveway and only one light on. At this point, I could only pray all had gone as planned and Julie had everyone gathered in the kitchen.

We let ourselves in the front door and as we walked into the den, a chorus of voices serenaded us from the kitchen. I knew Mama would be surprised, maybe even shocked, but I wasn't prepared for what happened next. For the first time in all of my forty-three years, I saw my mama cry.

For a moment, nobody knew how to respond, including me.

Nobody expected this from Googa—she had always been the pillar of strength in our family. At eighty-five, she was still considered be the most stalwart among us.

After what seemed like an eternity of awkward silence, movement erupted and everyone started talking at once. Mama sat down in a chair and someone handed her a glass of wine. As I scanned the room with my video camera, I noticed Margaret sitting quietly in a chair close to Mama's, taking it all in. She had a peaceful look on her face and I could tell that the situation hadn't been awkward to her at all. Margaret knew exactly how to respond. Without hesitation, she walked over to Mama and kissed her on the cheek.

"Happy Birthday, Mama," she said. "You're the best."

Truth

"HONEY, YOU'VE GOT MORE STATIC THAN a bad radio." The palm reader stared at my hands through bloodshot eyes. "See all these tiny crisscrossed lines? You've got all kinds of stuff going on here."

"Like what?" I asked. Now she had my attention.

"Somebody's been messing with your money," she responded with a serious look.

"No, I don't think so," I replied.

"Somebody in your family's messing with you then."

"No, not that either."

"Some man's been treatin' you bad, huh?"

"No, I'm sorry, that's not the case."

I felt bad for her. She looked like she'd been up all night and probably had a wicked hangover. I felt bad because I knew she was just trying to make an honest living.

I was in New Orleans for a conference and had ventured down to Jackson Square to have coffee and beignets and watch the sun come up. I was heading back to my hotel when she caught my eye—a large woman with stringy blond hair hanging out of a dirty bandana. She rested her head on a small table draped with a sign that read, *Lady Hawke.* Beer cans and cigarette butts littered the ground around her feet. Something about her

178

drew me in for a closer look, and then, just as I turned to leave, she raised up and smiled a toothless grin.

"Are you open?" I asked, not knowing the proper etiquette in these situations.

"I'm always open, honey. Sit down here," she said, pointing to a folding chair. "I was just catching a few winks, had a busy night last night."

Following her attempt to discover why my palms were covered with chaos, she sat quietly, pondering. Then, a proclamation, "You're just a bleeding heart, aren't you, honey? You've got to stop trying to save the world."

"Bingo!" I shouted. "Now you've hit the nail on the head."

She threw her head back and howled, "I knew it all along."

Lady Hawke went on for another thirty minutes or so, asking questions and telling tales. She had been married six times, the first four to men. That was her daughter over there, the tall pretty one. She worked at a restaurant, but liked hanging out with the street vendors.

Eventually, she got around to telling me that I was meant for a life of service and that I would help lots of people. She wasn't really sure how.

"How much do I owe you?" I asked after we'd visited a while longer.

"Oh, I just take donations, honey, anything from ten to thirty dollars. Whatever you feel inclined to give."

I placed a twenty dollar bill on the table. "I enjoyed it," I said.

She winked at me. "Don't you let anybody mess with you, you hear? You been messed with enough."

This woman had a kind spirit and what seemed to be a very old soul. Regardless of how she got to the truth about me, she uncovered it just the same, and she certainly peeled back the layers easier than I have. The journey for me has been a long one.

From a very young age, I had an awareness of trying to please everyone—my mother, my teachers, my friends. For as long as I can remember, I've felt a void, like something was wrong with me, something was missing. *I have to do more, I have to be more—*

smarter, prettier, sweeter—better at just about everything. I constantly compared myself to others and came up short.

As I got older, this translated into a reactive, victim-like attitude. I felt as if I had no control over what happened to me, as if other people and outside forces were creating all the circumstances in my life; as if *my* choices made no difference. Yet through all this chaos and struggle, somehow I knew there was a reason for Margaret's presence in my life, even if I couldn't explain it.

"I know I'm the person I am today because of Margaret," I said often, not knowing at all what it meant.

"She's been an incredible influence in my life," I repeated over and over again, knowing it to be true, without really understanding how or why.

I wasn't ready to receive the truth, but as the words poured out and the pages unfolded, everything began to shift. My life would take a dramatic turn and my writing would take on an entirely different meaning. Even though I started writing to tell Margaret's story, I know now that I can't finish without telling my own.

Healing

AT SOME POINT IN TIME, I probably would have described meeting Rebecca Hamm the same way I would describe meeting any other person in my life. I would have called it luck, or maybe a coincidence. I might have even said something like, "It was weird, she just showed up at my house."

Since meeting her, though, I would describe her presence in my life as nothing short of amazing. To call it a coincidence would lend credence to the belief that angels don't exist.

Simply put, Rebecca is the most light-filled person I have ever met. After talking with her for a couple of hours, I knew she was unlike any person I would ever know again. A cancer survivor and deeply spiritual being, she is a counselor by trade and an earth-angel by the grace of God. Her eyes and heart see only the goodness in others. Even though I was in her presence only a few short days, I vowed to keep in touch with her and knew our paths would cross again.

It was also no coincidence that I met Rebecca just as I was about to delve into the crux of my writing. In the months following our meeting, it seemed that ideas came to me daily and progress on the book was steady. At the same time, I was having more conversations with Mama, asking lots of questions about Margaret. It felt good to share this bond with my mother, to know her as a person, not just my parent.

Then, quite suddenly, I realized that time with Mama left me feeling sad and depressed, sometimes, even angry. I was also acutely aware of how difficult it was for me to accept Margaret's affection. I found myself pulling away from her hugs, as if her love was too much to bear. I felt guilty, ashamed, and very angry with myself. But then, to be honest, I had always been uncomfortable with Margaret's displays of affection toward me. The only difference now was that I had no choice but to acknowledge it.

At first, I did my best to push through the conflicting emotions and stay focused on my task—finishing the book. I soon realized that my way of dealing with my emotional state (ignoring it) wasn't working. The sadness remained, my writing began to suffer, and before long, I was devoid of ideas altogether. All I could focus on was pain.

Not sure which way to turn, I decided to call Rebecca. Gracious and humbled by my request, she offered to give me as much of her time as I needed. In the same way Dr. Rivers shared his gift with Mama, Rebecca shared hers with me, and I will be forever grateful.

It was through working with Rebecca that I began to understand the significance of Margaret's presence in my life, as well as the meaning of the difficult issues I had grappled with for years—the longing I felt as a child, the desire to please everyone, the struggle and self-doubt that plagued me throughout my adulthood—everything was finally coming to the surface.

The reason I felt such sadness, she told me, was because I felt angry about not getting enough attention from my parents when I was young. She continued, saying that whether it was true or not, I felt "unseen" by them, and that talking to Mama about Margaret conjured up all too familiar feelings of unworthiness. She explained that my response to these conversations was based on fear I felt as a child; that I was able, even at a very young age, to sense my mother's apprehension about raising a child with disabilities. "You reacted that," she said. "On some level, your heart knew what your mother was going through."

I sat transfixed, knowing that more powerful words regarding my relationship with my mother had never been spoken.

"And the reason I feel so uncomfortable when Margaret hugs me?" I asked.

"It's because you don't feel worthy of her adoration," said Rebecca. "You deny her love because of your anger and guilt. Margaret is a reflection of you, a way for you to see yourself the way God sees you," she continued. "But you've been taught to believe that unconditional love like hers doesn't exist."

I sat quietly, trying to take it all in.

"Don't analyze it," Rebecca said softly. "Just open your heart and receive. When Margaret hugs you, imagine God holding you in His arms."

The next time we spoke, I told Rebecca that I was able to accept one of Margaret's hugs; that I didn't pull away quite so quickly. I acknowledged that I was still having difficulty talking to Mama though, and that I felt frustrated when she couldn't seem to articulate how she was feeling, or remember something about Margaret or me when we were little. "I don't know why it's so hard for her to tell me how she felt about things," I complained.

"When you sit with the sadness or anger you feel after a conversation with your mother," Rebecca said, "you have to take Margaret out of the picture. Margaret may be the subject of your conversation, but your response has nothing to do with her. This is about you and your mother, and your writing has provided a way for both of you to heal."

At the mention of those words, I began to cry, a flood of emotion sweeping over me. Years of anger and resentment began to melt away and with each passing day, my heart opened a little more. No longer did I blame Mama for anything. No longer did I focus on what was or wasn't in my childhood. Finally, I was able to see my mother for the remarkable, courageous woman she is. *A chance to heal*, I thought. *That's* why I've felt compelled to write.

183

Light

WHEN I STARTED WRITING THINGS DOWN that December many years ago, I had only one goal in mind—to preserve my sister's memory. *I'll write some funny stories,* I thought. *People always want to hear stories about Margaret.*

And so I began to write, using only my memory to guide me. I didn't think about talking to Margaret's friends, her teachers, or even to Mama, for that matter; I was convinced I knew enough to tell the story myself.

Once my writing took a more serious turn, I began reading other books about people with Down syndrome, most of them written from a parent's point of view. It suddenly dawned on me that I knew very little about the events that transpired before I was born. As I opened a dialogue with my mother, a beautiful, touching story began to unfold; a story of courage, hope and inspiration; a story not just about my sister, but also about the person who has been her guardian, confidante, and lifelong advocate.

Learning this "story behind the story" has been a transformational experience. What hit me the hardest was the knowledge that my parents, and most especially my mother, had ever experienced pain or struggle of any kind. For as long as I can remember, I had regarded my mother as a force to be reckoned with—forthright, fearless and emotionally unflappable.

What I wasn't able to comprehend as a child, or even as a young adult, was that the shield of armor my mother bore was necessary for her survival. With the birth of a child with Down syndrome, her world was turned upside down. Not knowing what else to do, Mama made a contract with God: *If you think I'm capable of taking care of her, I'll dedicate my life to the cause.* In Mama's mind, she had been given a lifelong responsibility and she accepted her role without question.

Focusing all of her energy on the task at hand, Mama wasn't able to perceive the birth of a handicapped child as a blessing or special gift from God, she saw it as a duty. Mama had too much responsibility to become emotionally invested—after all, she had been entrusted with a significant task.

But for me, life was different. As the baby of the family, I saw my big sister in a totally different light. From the moment I was born, Margaret became my biggest fan and was never reserved in her displays of affection. With unbridled adoration, she nurtured me in ways that Mama never could. Mama focused on parenting, Margaret focused on showering me with love. Mama planted seeds, Margaret made sure they were watered.

Through my talks with Rebecca, I learned that the void created by the need to please my mother could now be filled through my writing, and that Margaret has given us all a chance to see ourselves in a more perfect light.

"You hold the gift of love in your family," she advised me. "In telling this story, you have an opportunity to bring your family closer together, to honor your mother for her courage and to heal the wounds that have separated you."

At once, I knew she was right. I felt it with every fiber of my being, a knowing that words could never explain. From that point forward, my writing changed and the story took on a life of its own. As I wrote, I began to realize that the universe cannot be controlled, and life, soul, spirit will move toward light, if it finds even one small crack through which to squeeze.

"You'll be amazed at how your life will be transformed when you accept that Margaret is an extension of God," Rebecca said. "She is your teacher and she's here to teach you unconditional love. Now all you have to do is accept the gift."

Author's Note

I MUST ADMIT THAT MANY TIMES throughout my life, I've wondered what it would be like to have a "normal" big sister—you know, someone you can talk to about your personal life or the guilt trips your parents sent you on over the years; someone to go to for advice or a shoulder to cry on; someone to tell you that no matter how bad things are, everything is going to be okay.

After writing this book, I realized that Margaret doesn't have to tell me or show me any of those things. She makes me conscious of them by her very existence. By the way her heart knows no judgment, no deceit, no hatred; by the incredible purity of her soul and the way she exemplifies the true meaning of love. I know that my sister Margaret is a beautiful, perfect example of all that's good in this world.

As my friend and I sat talking about the purpose our souls have on earth, she posed a thoughtful question: *What do you think Margaret's soul came here to do?*

I didn't have an immediate response, but then one day while I was sitting quietly, the answer presented itself: *She has come to show you the way.*

For most of us, life holds a great deal of uncertainty, but there is one thing about which I have no doubt—no matter what *my* soul came here to do, it came knowing that Margaret would be my guide, and for me, that alone has made the journey worthwhile.

Epilogue

Dear Daddy,

It's been a long time since we've talked. First of all, I want to say that I love you and miss you very much; I find it hard to believe that you left this world over twenty years ago.

I know we didn't spend much time together, Daddy, and a lot of that is my fault. I was young and foolish and took things for granted. I thought you would be around forever.

Secondly, I want to tell you that I'm writing a book. It's a book about our family, mostly about Mama and Margaret, but also about you, and I thought you should know. I wanted to put something down on paper so that generations of our family to come would know about Margaret and her relationship with Mama. I want them to know what a gift both of them are to our family. I know that you felt that way too, Daddy, you just had a hard time expressing it.

There are so many things to tell you about Margaret, that I don't even know where to begin. Her accomplishments are too numerous to list, but most importantly, what you should know is that she leads a full, happy life. She has lots of friends and she's constantly going somewhere or doing something fun. She's smart, loving, funny and kind, all the things you would want your daughter to be, not to mention, she's a wonderful big sister and a pretty terrific aunt.

I know you were upset when she was born, Daddy, but that's okay—you didn't know any other way to be. And when your boss told you to send her away, that must have been so confusing and frightening. Well, you don't have to worry anymore. You don't have to be afraid or ashamed of having a child who was disabled. You can rest peacefully knowing that you and Mama brought an angel into this world, an angel whose presence on this earth is affecting people's lives way beyond measure. As difficult as it was for you, I know you would be proud to be her father.

Well, here I am going on and on about Margaret and I'm sure you're wondering about Mama. That woman is amazing—she's still as smart, courageous and of course, stubborn as ever. Since you've been gone she's survived breast cancer, heart failure, and worst of all, me never getting married! But not once has she complained. I know that doesn't surprise you, though, you saw firsthand how she took on the responsibility of raising a child with disabilities with virtually no outside support. She's an inspiration to me and everyone who knows her and her beautiful smile can still light up a room.

We all miss you, Daddy, and there have been so many times that I thought about you and how proud you would've been if you'd been here. Like when Margaret made it all the way to the Special Olympics World Games for instance, or when she won three gold medals in one day at a state swim meet, or when your grandson was born (you're his namesake by the way), or when I graduated from Auburn with a master's degree. Each time, Mama said, "I wish your daddy was here to see this."

I have no doubt that you are with us though, Daddy, I know because I see it in Margaret's eyes and hear it in her laughter. When she puts her arms around me and tells me she loves me, I feel the warmth of your love as well as hers. I also see it in Jake's personality, how everyone who knows him can't help but like him.

So don't worry, Daddy, your spirit lives on in all of us, but be assured that it shines brightest in Margaret, your special child. She is a sweet, precious gift and she won't be forgotten, I promise.

Printed in the United States
35007LVS00002B/25-36

9 781413 756937